Intelligence Engineering

SECURITY AND PROFESSIONAL
INTELLIGENCE EDUCATION SERIES (SPIES)
Series Editor: Jan Goldman

In this post–September 11, 2001, era there has been rapid growth in the number of professional intelligence training and educational programs across the United States and abroad. Colleges and universities, as well as high schools, are developing programs and courses in homeland security, intelligence analysis, and law enforcement, in support of national security.

The Security and Professional Intelligence Education Series (SPIES) was first designed for individuals studying for careers in intelligence and to help improve the skills of those already in the profession; however, it was also developed to educate the public in how intelligence work is conducted and should be conducted in this important and vital profession.

1. *Communicating with Intelligence: Writing and Briefing in the Intelligence and National Security Communities*, by James S. Major. 2008.
2. *A Spy's Résumé: Confessions of a Maverick Intelligence Professional and Misadventure Capitalist*, by Marc Anthony Viola. 2008.
3. *An Introduction to Intelligence Research and Analysis*, by Jerome Clauser, revised and edited by Jan Goldman. 2008.
4. *Writing Classified and Unclassified Papers for National Security*, by James S. Major. 2009.
5. *Strategic Intelligence: A Handbook for Practitioners, Managers, and Users*, revised edition by Don McDowell. 2009.
6. *Partly Cloudy: Ethics in War, Espionage, Covert Action, and Interrogation*, by David L. Perry. 2009.
7. *Tokyo Rose / An American Patriot: A Dual Biography*, by Frederick P. Close. 2010.
8. *Ethics of Spying: A Reader for the Intelligence Professional*, edited by Jan Goldman. 2006.
9. *Ethics of Spying: A Reader for the Intelligence Professional*, Volume 2, edited by Jan Goldman. 2010.
10. *A Woman's War: The Professional and Personal Journey of the Navy's First African American Female Intelligence Officer*, by Gail Harris. 2010.
11. *Handbook of Scientific Methods of Inquiry for Intelligence Analysis*, by Hank Prunckun. 2010.
12. *Handbook of Warning Intelligence: Assessing the Threat to National Security*, by Cynthia Grabo. 2010.
13. *Keeping U.S. Intelligence Effective: The Need for a Revolution in Intelligence Affairs*, by William J. Lahneman. 2011.

14. *Words of Intelligence: An Intelligence Professional's Lexicon for Domestic and Foreign Threats, Second Edition*, by Jan Goldman. 2011.
15. *Counterintelligence Theory and Practice*, by Hank Prunckun. 2012.
16. *Balancing Liberty and Security: An Ethical Study of U.S. Foreign Intelligence Surveillance, 2001–2009*, by Michelle Louise Atkin. 2013.
17. *The Art of Intelligence: Simulations, Exercises, and Games*, edited by William J. Lahneman and Rubén Arcos. 2014.
18. *Communicating with Intelligence: Writing and Briefing in National Security*, by James S. Major. 2014.
19. *Scientific Methods of Inquiry for Intelligence Analysis, Second Edition*, by Hank Prunckun. 2014.
20. *Quantitative Intelligence Analysis: Applied Analytic Models, Simulations and Games*, by Edward Waltz. 2014.
21. *The Handbook of Warning Intelligence: Assessing the Threat to National Security—The Complete Declassified Edition*, by Cynthia Grabo and Jan Goldman, 2015.

To view the books on our website, please visit https://rowman.com/Action/SERIES/RL/SPIES or scan the QR code below.

Intelligence Engineering

Operating Beyond
the Conventional

Adam D. M. Svendsen

ROWMAN & LITTLEFIELD
Lanham • Boulder • New York • London

Published by Rowman & Littlefield
A wholly owned subsidiary of The Rowman & Littlefield Publishing Group, Inc.
4501 Forbes Boulevard, Suite 200, Lanham, Maryland 20706
www.rowman.com

Unit A, Whitacre Mews, 26-34 Stannary Street, London SE11 4AB

British Library Cataloguing in Publication Information Available

Library of Congress Cataloging-in-Publication Data Available

ISBN 978-1-4422-7664-2 (cloth : alk. paper)
ISBN 978-1-4422-7665-9 (pbk. : alk. paper)
ISBN 978-1-4422-7666-6 (electronic)

♾™ The paper used in this publication meets the minimum requirements of
American National Standard for Information Sciences—Permanence of Paper
for Printed Library Materials, ANSI/NISO Z39.48-1992.

Printed in the United States of America

Contents

Acknowledgments

No book can be written without thanking many people for all of their assistance and support in several varying forms. First and foremost, thanks go to my family, and especially to my parents, David and Penny Svendsen, for all of their support and to whom this book is dedicated. Thanks also go to all my friends and various colleagues, especially Salem Dandan, who have helped sustain me while I was undertaking the background research for this book and while I was developing the various frameworks and models that help underpin its content. Several of the 'functional intelligence studies'–associated ideas in this book have considerably benefited from many wide-ranging discussions and from their earlier presentation at, and via insightful feedback acquired from, 'scholar-practitioner'–related conferences I have participated in across (mainly) Europe during the years 2012–2016. Those conferences that deserve particular mention include the annual conferences of the International Society of Military Sciences (ISMS); the International Symposium on Military Operational Research (ISMOR); the Human Geography in Defence Engagement: Annual International Spatial Socio-Cultural Knowledge Workshops, organised as part of the UK Defence Academy and Cranfield University's Symposia at Shrivenham; the European conference of the International Association for Intelligence Education (IAFIE); and the conferences organised by the Romanian National Intelligence Academy (*Mihai Viteazul*). Special thanks also goes to Marie-Claire Antoine at Rowman & Littlefield and to the reviewers for helping me realise this project.

Adam D. M. Svendsen, PhD
@intstrategist
August 2016

Part I

WHERE WE ARE TODAY

Introduction

Intelligence Persists

Intelligence today continues to undergo significant changes and at a remarkable pace. Since completing the precursor studies to this book during early 2012—namely, *Understanding the Globalization of Intelligence* (2012) and *The Professionalization of Intelligence Cooperation: Fashioning Method Out of Mayhem* (2012), as well as drawing on *Intelligence Cooperation and the War on Terror: Anglo-American Security Relations after 9/11* (2010)—much of note has happened to intelligence. An update and a suggestion of where to go next is now warranted, with this book forming a contribution.

CURRENT LANDSCAPE

While naturally not everything can be covered within this book, several accomplished analysts of intelligence have continued to publish much interesting work focused on notable themes, such as 'intelligence elsewhere'.[1] That work has added in a complementary manner to many of the observations that were introduced and discussed in my original, earlier studies and on which the findings of this book, developed over the years 2012–2016, now aim to build. During 2012, security analyst Glen Segell reminded us that when taken at its broadest,

> information exchange is M4IS2: multiagency, multinational, multidisciplinary, multidomain information sharing and sense making; and the eight entities that do M4IS2 are commerce, academic, government, civil society, media, law enforcement, military and non-government/non-profit.[2]

Much intelligence-related work over the past few years has effectively re-flected that trend.

Well-established and long-standing Anglo-American intelligence and security interactions, extending to UKUSA relations, have also been much discussed in recent years. Involving some revisitation, that discussion has included the charting of the continual evolution and development of those relations over different timeframes and in varying directions.[3] More broadly, those entities—together with other transatlantic and partnerships further afield—have been opened up to both substantial and considerably wider public scrutiny, including to an unprecedented extent. For many participants, the situation remains (1) not always comfortable and welcomed; and, more disappointingly, (2) often subject to not-so-well-focused or balanced commentary and addressing.

To date, these developments have been especially apparent in the wake of the high-profile, so-called revelations coming from former U.S. Central Intelligence Agency/National Security Agency (CIA/NSA) and private sector computer administrator contractor Edward Snowden. Occurring almost literally by the (virtually unable to be adequately verified) terabyte load and arguably going beyond merely legitimate whistleblower-attributable activities, together with attracting much controversy in part due to their large scope and substantial frequency, his unlawful and damaging series of leaks have mainly consisted of his provision of a mass of secret intelligence material that he began distributing to the international media and other organisations since early June 2013. Those activities occurred after Snowden downloaded approximately 1.7 million classified documents in breach of his privileged insider-access to NSA servers and before his finding of sanctuary in Russia, from where he has continued to give interviews and provide further, frequently questionable commentary to accompany his series of leaks.[4]

Far too many questions still remain. As former U.S. intelligence practitioner Mark Lowenthal has noted in his preface to the sixth edition of his book *Intelligence: From Secrets to Policy* (2015), 'The Manning and Snowden leaks have had widespread repercussions, and these are discussed, albeit with the following caution: *This leaked intelligence remains and should be considered classified, despite the fact that it has been leaked*'. As a result, there are persistent dilemmas that need to be adequately taken into account. Lowenthal continues, 'Therefore, I cannot discuss the details of some of these leaks or comment on their veracity unless there are official comments on the subject'.[5]

A first caution emerges: Prevailing conjecture should not be taken for fact. Substantial uncertainty thus continues, and some areas continue to be 'fenced-off' for a variety of reasons, such as continuing secrecy requirements, even if, currently, 'hiding in plain sight' might now be more effective. Notably, we should not ignore or overlook associated warnings. Indeed, especially since from around 2008 concern has existed that rapidly and diversely developing processes—such as the 'globalisation of intelligence'—had to be carefully managed in contemporary contexts or there would be some degree of tangible fallout, characterised as 'negative consequences'.[6]

Little can be taken at merely face-value. Subsequently, along with other areas of intelligence-related enterprise and endeavour—and relating to diverse jobs, missions, and operations-to-other projects, however precisely scaled— we still see that (at least generally) intelligence-related phenomena, including the central mechanism of intelligence liaison, continue to cut both ways. Acting as double-edged swords, these developments have led to equally vexing and fascinating effects and outcomes that have continued to both challenge and aid employers and analysts alike.[7] Clearly, whatever we might think or experience, enhanced intelligence relevance endures.

CONTEMPORARY TERRAIN CONTOURS

Relating to the more theoretical-ranging insights provided by the studies on which this book now builds, since 2012 greater work has been accomplished clarifying the complex links and nexuses to currently developing 'system of systems' or 'federation of systems' concepts. Overall, these constructs are collectively encapsulated and rationalised as System of Systems Dynamics (SoSD). These multi-faceted SoSD approaches, at their broadest involving System of Systems Analysis (SoSA) and System of Systems Engineering (SoSE) constructs, are currently emerging in their application in the intelligence, security, and defence domains of human and technical/technological activity. That trend includes SoSD being embedded via their greater consolidation within military, law enforcement (policing), and emergency/crisis management (civil protection) work.[8]

Extending beyond just single entities, SoSD involve multiple intelligence disciplines (multi-INTs) and all-source-intelligence-associated collection and analysis/assessment efforts. These, in turn, occur both in and across several multifunctional operations to special operations (MFOs to SpecOps/SOs) that range over a multitude of varying war-to-peace environments during an overall era of globalised strategic risk, and as so-called hybrid or non-linear situations continue to manifest themselves in notably ambiguous manners. This creates much complexity spanning both #2 Intelligence (e.g., G/J2) and #3 Operations (e.g., G/J3) areas of military and further-extending civilian activity, changing their proximities and interactions in several diverse ways. Various agendas and the revolution in military affairs (RMA) continue.[9]

Greater light has also been shone elsewhere. Relevant particularly to the more empirically ranging case-study material presented in the earlier studies and companion volumes to this book, further examination of critical 'intelligence *and* policy' and 'intelligence analysis *and* science', together with 'intelligence *and* Special Operational Forces (SOF)' themes, has undergone substantial engagement since early 2012.[10] Many prominent intelligence management, control, and usage considerations and concerns, alongside the articulation of a multitude of different agendas, were similarly still very much in evidence during 2015–2016.[11] In July 2015, international agreement was additionally reached on Iran's nuclear programme, opening up further intriguing intelligence-related developments.[12]

More widely, the 'resilience' concept has likewise continued to develop, becoming more established particularly in safety, disaster, and crisis-management-associated areas.[13] When confronting both natural and manmade catastrophic events, emergency-planning-related resilience stays crucial. This was substantially reinforced both during and after the horrific attacks that took place in 2015 and 2016 in Paris, Ankara, Beirut, Istanbul, Brussels, Nice, and Munich, over the skies of the Sinai Desert, and beyond, and as these crimes-to-declared-'acts of war' remained manifest.[14]

AND SO THIS BOOK

A more focused approach is required. As this book underlines, (1) intelligence continues to move beyond being merely a combination of the 'arts' and 'sciences' and it continues to extend into 'engineering' realms, including SoSE approaches and their greater refinement, such as via social engineering and similar activities, together with a better tackling of questions of response to pressing *What next?* queries; (2) a mode of functional intelligence studies (FIS), with built-in practical and pragmatic communicable utility, is achievable in a constructive 'scholar-practitioner' or 'inky-fingered soldier'—even 'poacher-turned-gamekeeper'—manner; and (3) notable intelligence end-user/customer criteria relating to the qualities of specificity, timeliness, accuracy, relevance, and clarity (STARC) remain of enduring importance and are worth keeping at the forefront. This is especially important as decision- and policy-makers, practitioners to other operatives and operators all strive to find the next global-ranging reference points for management to governance.[15]

Intelligence optimisation helps. The further extension of analysis work (breaking down and answering the *What is it?* queries), and deeper-ranging connective and synthesising assessment/estimate efforts (addressing the building- and sense-making-related questions of *What does it mean? Why?*

and *So what?*)—clearly continues to retain much demonstrable value in contemporary circumstances. Many participants stand to benefit in the future as intelligence tradecraft and its skillsets are advanced through improved teaching and training.[16] With regard to more specific intelligence *and* policing contexts, and with at least some simultaneous applicability to other domains of intelligence endeavour, worthy themes to reiterate include

the need for increased training; a realisation that [(as given in this example)] the policing setting is changing to one of greater networks and pluralism; the need for a strategic perspective; and finally the importance of a close relationship between [(again as highlighted in this example)] police leadership and analysts.[17]

A MANIFESTO FOR INTELLIGENCE ENGINEERING (IE) AND OPERATING BEYOND THE CONVENTIONAL

Maintaining the above types of elevated statuses is necessary, especially as significant, full-spectrum-ranging, intelligence-related events and developments continue to rapidly go forward and undergo much challenging and disruptive change. Simultaneously, vital imperatives-to-initiatives for maintaining crucial 'edges' and for keeping ahead of the curve of events and developments in intelligence, defence, and security enterprises require both promulgation and prolongation calibrated on sustainable and critically sharp bases. The benefits are substantial if we keep intelligence dynamics and all of their associated qualities firmly in sight. This is essential for moving forward in a constructive and productive manner as the future quickly unfolds.[18]

Ultimately today, greater design and shaping phenomena, such as the main focus of this book, intelligence engineering (IE), assume a more central position. Again, going beyond merely the arts and sciences—which are traditionally associated with intelligence and its work—the development and extension of IE emerges as a useful place for next steps. Actively encouraging the re-invigoration of much-challenged contemporary intelligence, together with advancing greater understanding, an introduction to IE now follows. Operating beyond the conventional requires further scrutiny amidst implementation.

NOTES

1. See esp. P.H.J. Davies and K.C. Gustafson, eds., *Intelligence Elsewhere* (Washington, DC: Georgetown University Press, 2013); R.J. Aldrich and J. Kasuku, 'Escaping from American intelligence: Culture, ethnocentrism and the Anglosphere',

International Affairs 88, 5 (September 2012); Z. Shiraz, 'Drugs and dirty wars: Intelligence cooperation in the global South', *Third World Quarterly* 34, 10 (2013); see chapters in R. Dover, M.S. Goodman and C. Hillebrand, eds., *Routledge Companion to Intelligence Studies* (London: Routledge, 2013); G. Hastedt, 'Book review: "Understanding the Globalization of Intelligence", Adam N. [*sic*] M. Svendsen', *Journal of Contingencies and Crisis Management* 21, 2 (June 2013), pp. 25–26; I. Duyvesteyn et al., eds., *The Future of Intelligence* (London: Routledge, 2014); W. Bułhak and T. Wegener Friis, eds., *Need to Know* (Odense: UPSDk, 2014); see also texts cited in A.D.M. Svendsen, 'Contemporary intelligence innovation in practice', *Defence Studies* 15, 2 (2015), pp. 05–23; M. Matina and B. Blanchard, 'China says defence spending pace to slow, to improve intelligence', Reuters (5 March 2016). With a Europe/EU focus, C. Kaunert and S. Leonard, eds., *European Security, Terrorism, and Intelligence* (Basingstoke, UK: Palgrave Macmillan, 2013); K. Clerix, 'Ilkka Salmi, the EU's spymaster', *Mondiaal Nieuws* (March 2014); B. Fägersten, 'European intelligence cooperation', ch. 8 in Duyvesteyn et al., eds., *The Future of Intelligence*; 'EU doesn't need a CIA—But better intelligence would help', EurActiv.com (16 October 2015); 'Intelligence and decision-making within the common foreign and security policy', *European Policy Analysis* (Stockholm: Swedish Institute for European Policy Studies, 2015); and 'For EU eyes only? Intelligence and European security', *European Union Institute for Security Studies Issue Brief 8* (March 2016); B. de Graaff and J.M. Nyce with C. Locke, *Handbook of European Intelligence Cultures* (Lanham, MD: Rowman & Littlefield, 2016); A. Gruszczak, *Intelligence Security in the European Union* (London: Springer, 2016); B. Caspit, 'Why Europe must unify its intelligence networks', *Al-Monitor* (23 March 2016); A. Soufan, 'Terrorists cross borders with ease: It's vital that intelligence does too', *Guardian*; B. Tigner, 'EU members to accelerate standing counter- terrorism proposals, including PNR', IHS Jane's 360; H. Jacobsen, 'EU justice ministers step up intelligence sharing after Brussels attacks'; and C. Mihai, 'Romanian president lauds intelligence services, says country 'Is safe',' EurActiv.com (24–25/30 March 2016).

2. G. Segell, 'Book review: *International Intelligence Cooperation and Accountability*', *Political Studies Review*, 10, 3 (2012), pp. 10–11; J. Richards, *A Guide to National Security* (Oxford: Oxford University Press, 2012); A.P. Waddell, 'Cooperation and integration among Australia's national security community', *Studies in Intelligence*, 59, 3 (September 2015), pp. 5–34; A. Corrin, 'How BICES-X facilitates global intelligence', *C4ISRNet* (11 February 2016).

3. See, for example, P.H.J. Davies, *Intelligence and Government in Britain and the United States* (Westport, CT: Praeger, 2012); M.S. Goodman, 'Evolution of a relationship—The foundations of Anglo-American intelligence sharing', *Studies in Intelligence*, 59, 2 (2015); A.D.M. Svendsen, '"Strained" relations? Evaluating contemporary Anglo-American intelligence and security co-operation', ch. 8 in S. Marsh and A. Dobson, eds., *Anglo-American Relations: Contemporary Perspectives* (London: Routledge, 2012); R. Jeffreys-Jones, *In Spies We Trust* (Oxford: Oxford University Press, 2013); M. Hosenball, 'U.S., Britain consider letting spy agencies, police seek email, chat data from companies', Reuters (5 February 2016); E. Nakashima, 'Lynch: Wiretap agreement with Britain would protect privacy, human rights', *Wash-*

ington Post (1 March 2016); R.J. Aldrich and R. Cormac, *The Black Door* (London: Collins, 2016); C. Walton, 'Little Britain: Brexit and the UK-US special intelligence relationship', *Prospect Magazine* (10 August 2016). For 'Readers', see L.K. Johnson and J.J. Wirtz, eds., *Intelligence*, 4th ed. (Oxford: Oxford University Press, 2014); R.J. Aldrich, W.K. Wark, and C. Andrew, eds., *Secret Intelligence*, 2nd ed. (London: Routledge, 2016).

4. For commentary, see A.D.M. Svendsen, 'Buffeted not busted: The UKUSA 'five eyes' after Snowden', *e-ir.info* (8 January 2014); 'Edward Snowden: Leaks that exposed US spy programme', BBC (17 January 2014); L. Harding, *The Snowden Files* (New York: Vintage, 2014); 'Edward Snowden joins Twitter and follows NSA', BBC (29 September 2015); E. MacAskill, 'Edward Snowden: US has not offered me plea deal', *Guardian* and P. Taylor, 'Edward Snowden: Man at the eye of a storm', BBC (5 October 2015); J. Grierson, 'Edward Snowden would be willing to return to US for fair trial', *Guardian* (21 February 2016); J. Hattem, 'Snowden: FBI's stance in Apple case is 'horses—'', *The Hill* (8 March 2016); F. Hill, 'Putin: The one-man show the West doesn't understand', *Bulletin of the Atomic Scientists*, 72, 3 (2016), p. 142; F. Jacobs, 'How Russia works on intercepting messaging apps', *Bellingcat* (30 April 2016); 'Edward Snowden: "Governments can reduce our dignity to that of tagged animals"', *Guardian*; J. Hattem, 'Snowden cheers on increasing pace of government leaks'; and K.B. Williams, 'Internal NSA newsletters leaked by Snowden published online', *The Hill* (3/16 May 2016); S. Hennessey, 'VICE's vice: Snowden scoop promises fire, doesn't even muster smoke', *Lawfare* (8 June 2016); M. Weinger, 'Snowden's impact fades after three years'; 'The Snowden fact-check', *The Cipher Brief*; and J. Goldsmith, 'Three years later: How Snowden helped the U.S. intelligence community', *Lawfare* (5–6 June 2016); 'Sometimes the only moral decision is to break the law,' Murmur.dk (28 June 2016). On 'insider threats', R. Yasin, 'ODNI task force and DoD partner to fight insider threats', *C4ISRNet* (18 February 2016); A. Sternstein, 'What's your 'insider threat score"?', *Defense One* (2 May 2016); M.G. Gelles, *Insider Threat* (Oxford: Butterworth-Heinemann, 2016); E. Lake, 'Intel whistle-blowers fear government won't protect them', Bloomberg (8 March 2016); S. Aftergood, 'Punishing leaks through administrative channels', *FAS Secrecy News* (3 May 2016); M. Hertsgaard, 'Opinion: Whistle-Blower, Beware', *New York Times* (26 May 2016); K. Lowry, 'Closing the insider threat loop with authority', *Federal Times*; and J. Bamford, 'Commentary: Evidence points to another Snowden at the NSA', Reuters (15/26 August 2016); C. Savage, 'Obama administration set to expand sharing of data that NSA intercepts', *New York Times* (25 February 2016); M.V. Hayden, *Playing to the Edge* (New York: Penguin, 2016); S. Slick, 'Chalked spikes and Bush-era intelligence', *Lawfare* (28 March 2016); L. Stigsgaard Nissen, 'Denmark's spy agency is creating a training academy for hackers', *Quartz* (9 April 2016); T. Risen, 'When is NSA hacking ok?' *U.S. News & World Report* (23 May 2016).

5. M.M. Lowenthal, *Intelligence: From Secrets to Policy*, 6th ed. (Washington, DC: CQ, 2015), p. 15 (emphasis added); 'Chelsea Manning faces discipline for prison suicide attempt—Lawyers', Reuters (29 July 2016).

6. A.D.M. Svendsen, *Understanding the Globalization of Intelligence* (Basingstoke, UK: Palgrave Macmillan, 2012), p. 88; A.D.M. Svendsen, 'The globalization

of intelligence since 9/11: Frameworks and operational parameters', *Cambridge Review of International Affairs*, 21, 1 (March 2008); and A.D.M. Svendsen, 'The globalization of intelligence since 9/11: The optimization of intelligence liaison arrangements', *International Journal of Intelligence and CounterIntelligence*, 21, 4 (December 2008); see also C. Pazzanese, 'Hiding money in plain sight', *Harvard Gazette* (1 April 2016); E. Knowles, 'Britain's culture of no comment', *Remote Control Briefing* (4 July 2016).

7. See, e.g., as discussed in Svendsen, *Understanding the Globalization of Intelligence*, p. 70, p.155; N. Syeed, 'CIA cyber official sees data flood as both godsend and danger', Bloomberg; A. Boyd, 'DIA cyber officer profiles global threat actors'; and M. Pomerleau, 'Info-sharing hurdles hinders alliance partnerships', *C4ISRNet* (1/8 August 2016).

8. D. Jordan et al., *Understanding Modern Warfare*, 2nd ed. (Cambridge: Cambridge University Press, 2016), pp. 29–31; for more, see, e.g., A.D.M. Svendsen, 'An intelligence-engineering framework for defence engagement considerations', paper presented at the *Human Geography in Defence Engagement: 9th Annual International Spatial Socio-Cultural Knowledge Workshop* (UK Defence Academy and Cranfield University, Shrivenham, UK, May 2016); reports, e.g., F.M.J. Lichacz and R. Jassemi-Zargani, *Human Factors and Intelligence, Surveillance, and Reconnaissance* (Ottawa, Canada: Defence Research and Development Canada, April 2016).

9. See, notably, A.D.M. Svendsen, 'Advancing 'defence-in-depth': Intelligence and systems dynamics', *Defense & Security Analysis*, 31, 1 (2015), pp. 8–73; Svendsen, 'Contemporary intelligence innovation in practice', 105–23; R.M. Clark and W.L. Mitchell, *Target-Centric Network Modeling* (Washington, DC: CQ, 2015); B. Connable, *Military Intelligence Fusion for Complex Operations* (Washington, DC: Rand Corporation, 2012); A. Dupont and W.J. Reckmeyer, 'Australia's national security priorities: Addressing strategic risk in a globalised world', *Australian Journal of International Affairs*, 66, 1 (2012); J. Schroefl et al., eds., *Hybrid and Cyber War as Consequences of the Asymmetry* (Frankfurt: Peter Lang, 2011); D.E. Tromblay, 'The intelligence studies essay: "Hybrid warfare" at home, Asymmetric tactics are not just used in Ukraine, they are employed against the United States, and have been for quite some time', *Lawfare* (29 August 2016); see also A.D.M. Svendsen, 'Making it "STARC"! Proposed future ways forward for contemporary military & special operations intelligence & knowledge work', conference paper, *International Symposium on Military Operational Research* (22 July 2015); similar insights in ch. 3. Also advanced as part of the Global University Alliance's 'The Intelligence-domain System of Systems Dynamics Reference Content (SoSD)' project; A.D.M. Svendsen, 'International intelligence liaison: A primer', *Romanian Journal of Intelligence Studies* (2016); J.A. Kringen, 'Keeping watch on the world', *Studies in Intelligence*, 59, 3 (September 2015), pp. 1–10; B. Rosenberg and J. Edwards, 'How SOSE&I is synchronizing Army IT efforts', *C4ISRNet* (28 March 2016); G. Jennings, 'Lockheed Martin to progress USAF's "system-of-systems" effort', IHS Jane's 360 (24 August 2016); D.E. Sanger, '"Shadow brokers" leak raises alarming question: Was the N.S.A. hacked?' *New York Times*; J. Vijayan, 'Russia emerges as prime suspect in apparent NSA hack', *CSMPasscode*; and K.

Conger, 'Cisco and Fortinet say vulnerabilities disclosed in "NSA hack" are legit', Tech Crunch (16–17 August 2016).

10. W. Agrell and G.F. Treverton, *National Intelligence and Science* (Oxford: Oxford University Press, 2015); S.E. Dudley, 'Why "science" alone isn't enough for setting environmental policy', Reuters (2 October 2015); A.D.M. Svendsen, 'Sharpening SOF tools, their strategic use and direction', *Defence Studies*, 14, 3 (2014), pp. 284–309; W.L. Mitchell, 'Building a componential Danish SOF for a global SOF network', *FAK Brief* (Copenhagen: Royal Danish Defense College, 2014); L. Robinson, *One Hundred Victories* (New York: Public Affairs, 2013); K. Dilanian, 'CIA, special ops cooperate to kill extremists in Syria, Iraq', Associated Press (28 September 2015); J. Moran, 'Assessing SOF transparency and accountability', *Remote Control Report* (4 July 2016); Lt-Col. A. Lysgård (NOR), 'The Evolution of the Global SOF Enterprise from a Partner Perspective', *JSOU Occasional Paper* (2016); A. Powell, 'Advice from SOF on the Use of SOF for the Next Administration', *CNA* (2016); A.D.M. Svendsen, 'Introducing RESINT', *International Journal of Intelligence and CounterIntelligence*, 26, 4 (2013), pp. 777–94.

11. See, e.g., G. Miller, 'Former CIA officials release book defending agency interrogations', *Washington Post*; and C. Johnson, 'Rights group slams DOJ's "inconsistent" response to Senate torture report', NPR (8/22 September 2015); C.M. Poplin, 'What's in the CIA's note to the reader on the SSCI torture report?' *Lawfare* (11 February 2016); J. Gerstein, 'Appeals court won't order release of "torture report"', *Politico*; J. Hattem, 'CIA watchdog "accidentally destroyed" copy of "torture report"', *The Hill*; and M. Isikoff, 'Senate report on CIA torture is one step closer to disappearing', Yahoo! News (13/16 May 2016); G. Miller, K. DeYoung, and J. Tate, 'Newly released CIA files expose grim details of agency interrogation program', *Washington Post*; and J. Hattem, 'CIA considered requesting advance immunity for enhanced interrogations', *The Hill* (14 June 2016); R. Norton-Taylor, 'Britain's failure to come clean over rendition is scandalous—Tory MP'; and R. Evans, 'CPS upholds decision not to charge over MI6 role in Libyans' rendition', *Guardian* (25 July/5 August 2016); H. Moynihan, 'UK drone strike on ISIS raises legal questions', *Chatham House* (15 September 2015); T. Kutsch, 'New leak of US intelligence highlights contours of drone program', *Al Jazeera* (15 October 2015); A. Corrin, 'Officials deny ISIS intelligence reports were altered', *C4ISRnet* (10 September 2015); M. Mazzetti and M. Apuzzo, 'Military analyst again raises red flags on progress in Iraq', *New York Times*; and R. Tomes, 'On the politicization of intelligence', *War on the Rocks* (23/29 September 2015); R. Chesney, 'Rendition fallout: Former CIA officer convicted in absentia by Italy possibly arrested in Portugal', *Lawfare*; and K. Dilanian, 'Army intelligence system said down during hospital attack', Associated Press (8/20 October 2015); D. De Luce, 'Did the Pentagon cook the books on its Afghanistan intel?' *Foreign Policy* (19 November 2015); 'Iraq Inquiry: Chilcot Report to be published on 6 July'; and 'Iraq Inquiry: Why has the report taken so long?' BBC (9 May 2016); see also related discussion and further 2016 sources in ch. 5. On intelligence management, U.S. Office of the Director of National Intelligence, 'DNI Unveils 2014 National Intelligence Strategy', no. 40-14 (17 September 2014); U.S. Office of the Director of National Intelligence, *National Intelligence Strategy (NIS)*

of the United States of America 2014 (September 2014). The ODNI's Information Sharing Environment Office has continued its 'nationalization of intelligence' work, covering diverse areas such as 'interoperability' and 'standards'—for more information, visit www.ise.gov. For changes the UK Intelligence and Security Committee (ISC) has undergone in recent years, including the ISC becoming (slightly) more accessible to the public, visit http://isc.independent.gov.uk/.

12. See, e.g., A. Soufan, 'Did Iran give up the Khobar Towers terrorist?' *Foreign Policy* (8 September 2015); T. Erdbrink and D.E. Sanger, 'Atomic agency defends how Iran collected evidence at secret base', *New York Times*; and 'White House sees signs Iran cooperating in IAEA nuclear inspections', Reuters (21–22 September 2015); A.D.M. Svendsen, 'Making arms control "smarter"? The importance of intelligence', *Utrikes Perspektiv* (October 2015), pp. 56–57; A. Nader, 'Commentary: New era with Iran? Not so fast', Rand Corporation; J. Pecquet, 'Will IAEA be able to verify Iran's nuclear program?' *Al-Monitor*; and M. Hadjicostis, 'Israel says Iran building terror network in Europe, US', Associated Press (23–24 February 2016); S. Orr, 'After the Iran nuclear deal: Challenges and opportunities', Rand Corporation; and R. Nephew, 'Devil in the details? Why the latest IAEA report kerfuffle is overblown', Brookings Institution (3/8 March 2016); 'Russia-Iranian missile tests do not violate U.N. resolution: Interfax', Reuters (30 March 2016); R. Rampton, 'Obama says will take time to bring Iran back into world economy', Reuters; and 'Iran's post-sanctions strategy', Soufan Group (1/11 April 2016); M. Campbell, 'How Congress can prevent a nuclear Iran', *Georgetown Security Studies Review* (15 May 2016); W. Bowen et al., *Living on the Edge* (Basingstoke, UK: Palgrave Macmillan, 2016); 'The Iran deal, one year out: What Brookings experts are saying', Brookings Institute; and P. Goldschmidt, 'Undermining JCPOA not in best interest of any party', Carnegie Endowment for International Peace (14/20 July 2016); R. Gladstone, 'Iran's top leader distances himself from nuclear pact, which he once supported'; D.E. Sanger, 'How an Iranian's spy saga ends, 6 years later: He's executed', *New York Times*; N. Wadhams and A. Capaccio, 'Iran improving Cyber abilities since nuclear deal, pentagon says', Bloomberg; 'Iran's expanding strategic reach', Soufan Group; 'Iran deploys Russian-made S-300 missiles at its Fordow nuclear site—TV', Reuters; and R. Gladstone, 'Iran arrests person linked to negotiations on nuclear deal', *New York Times* (1/7/9/24/29 August 2016).

13. See, e.g., D. Chandler, *Resilience* (London: Routledge, 2014); C. Fjäder, 'The nation-state, national security and resilience in the age of globalisation', *Resilience*, 2, 2 (2014), pp. 114–29; J. Rodin, *The Resilience Dividend* (London: Profile, 2015); Y. Sheffi, *The Power of Resilience* (Cambridge, MA: MIT Press, 2015); J. Lloyd, 'Opinion: The three gravest threats facing our world', Reuters (18 October 2015); M. Konnikova, 'How people learn to become resilient', *New Yorker*; and '100RC Network Exchange Program', *100 Resilient Cities* (11/23 February 2016); J. Shea, 'Resilience: A core element of collective defence', *NATO Review* (April 2016); 'Resilience of vulnerable communities to be enhanced', *Jamaica Observer*; W. Feiden, 'Small opportunity cities: Transforming small post-Industrial cities into resilient communities', German Marshall Fund of the United States; H. Kletter, 'Defining resilience', Oxford University Press blog (27–29 April 2016); C. Rye, 'Going local in aid will help build

disaster resilience', Reuters; and 'Developing a roadmap to resilience', Bloomberg (27 May 2016); D. Dobrygowski, 'Why is everyone talking about cyber resilience?' World Economic Forum; J. Fiksel, 'Attack in Nice exposes once again that our modern society lacks resilience', *The Conversation*; A. Bergin, 'The forgotten actor in Australia's counterterrorism plans', *The Strategist* (8/19 July/12 August 2016); A. Burgess et al., eds., *Routledge Handbook of Risk Studies* (London: Routledge, 2016); 'Disasters claim fewer lives this year but cost insurers more—Swiss Re', Reuters; B. Duffy, M. Quigley, and M. Sandiford, 'Italy's deadly earthquake is the latest in a history of destruction', *The Conversation*; and 'Which countries are most at risk of disasters?' Reuters (18/24/25 August 2016).

14. 'Hollande: Paris attacks were an "act of war" by Islamic State', *Defense News*; I. Anthony, 'Cities and security', www.sipri.org (14–15 November 2015); 'Two suicide bombers hit Hezbollah bastion in Lebanon, 43 killed', Reuters (12 November 2015); 'Exclusive—Investigators "90 percent sure" bomb downed Russian plane', Reuters (8 November 2015); M. Rowling, 'Global action too slow to curb rising risks—Ex-UN disaster chief', Reuters (11 January 2016); 'Ankara car bomb heralds Turkey's widening terror war', *Daily Beast*; 'Two attacks and two terror trends', Soufan Group (14 March 2016); P. Tremblay, 'Istanbul residents retreat from public spaces following latest attack', *Al-Monitor* (20 March 2016); P. Blenkinsop and F. Guarascio, 'Attacks on Brussels airport, metro kill at least 30', Reuters; J. Burke, 'Brussels attacks: Were they revenge for Abdeslam's arrest?' *Guardian* (22 March 2016); W. McCants, 'How Western Europe became ISIS's favorite battleground', *Time*; K.J. Greenberg, 'Brussels bombings are a sign of Islamic State's panic', Reuters; D. Byman, 'What the Brussels attacks tell us about the state of ISIS and Europe today', *Lawfare*; L. Sly, 'In Syria and Iraq, the Islamic State is in retreat on multiple fronts', *Washington Post*; J. Meyer et al., 'Dozens of terror plots thwarted across Europe, say officials', NBC; 'Brussels and the difficulties in connecting the dots'; and 'Resilience and the terror threat in Europe', Soufan Group (23–24/30 March 2016); T. Escritt, 'Belgium largest source of European fighters in Syria per head—Study', Reuters (1 April 2016); D. Byman, 'Europe vs. America: Comparing the terrorism threat', *Lawfare* (3 April 2016); S. Hamid, 'Why jihadists fight', Brookings Institution; 'Answering the Islamic State's call to terror', Soufan Group (14–15 June 2016); A. Breeden, 'Attacker in Nice plotted for months and had accomplices, French prosecutor says', *New York Times* (21 July 2016); M.L. Kelly, 'A summer of terrorism points to the limits of counterterrorism', NPR (24 July 2016); 'A week of terror in Germany', Soufan Group; 'Germany attacks: What is going on?' BBC (25 July 2016); 'France church attack: Priest killed in hostage taking near Rouen', BBC; A. Faiola and G. Witte, 'Amateur terror attacks may mark a new chapter in the ISIS war in Europe', *Washington Post*; P. Apps, 'Commentary: How much worse could 2016 get?' Reuters (26 July 2016); H. Horn, 'How ISIS is shaking up transatlantic views on surveillance and counter-terrorism', *Defense One*; 'Belgian police attacker shot and killed in Charleroi', BBC; 'Special report: A new war on terror', Soufan Group; 'Germany's rising terror threat', Soufan Group; 'Germany in new anti-terror plan to thwart Islamist militants', BBC; N. Lalwani and S. Winter-Levy, 'Here's why terrorist suicide attacks are increasing: They attract rewards from ISIS and al-Qaeda',

Washington Post; and W. Chalk, S. Maybin, and P. Brown, 'Terror deaths in Western Europe at highest level since 2004', BBC (August 2016).

15. See also, e.g., J. Jang, J. McSparren, and Y. Rashchupkina, 'Global governance: Present and future', *Palgrave Communications*, 2, 15045 (2016); C. May, 'Who's in charge? Corporations as institutions of global governance', *Palgrave Communications*, 1, 15042 (2015); A. Danchev, *On Good and Evil and the Grey Zone* (Edinburgh: Edinburgh University Press, 2016); W. Durch et al., 'Just security and the crisis of global governance', *Survival*, 58, 4 (2016), pp. 95–112; F. Fukuyama, 'Reflections on Chinese governance', *Journal of Chinese Governance*, 1, 3 (2016), pp. 379–91; D. Byman, 'Five tips for policy relevance', *Lawfare* (12 June 2016); D. Byman and M. Kroenig, 'Reaching beyond the ivory tower: A how to manual', *Security Studies*, 25, 2 (2016), pp. 289–319. For the 'STARC' criteria, see W.M. Hall and G. Citrenbaum, *Intelligence Collection* (Santa Barbara, CA: Praeger Security International, 2012), p. 81; see also W.M. Hall and G. Citrenbaum, *Intelligence Analysis* (Santa Barbara, CA: Praeger Security International, 2010); A.D.M. Svendsen, '"Making it STARC"!'

16. See, inter alia, J. Richards, *The Art and Science of Intelligence Analysis* (Oxford: Oxford University Press, 2010); G. Madhavan, 'Irrational humans need engineers, not economists', *Wired* (30 September 2015); A.D.M. Svendsen, 'Introducing RESINT', pp. 777–94; A.D.M. Svendsen, 'Collective intelligence (COLINT)' in G. Moore, ed., *Encyclopedia of U.S. Intelligence* (New York: CRC Press, 2014); A.D.M. Svendsen, 'Advancing "Defence-in-depth"', p. 59; R.M. Clark, *Intelligence Analysis*, 4th ed. (Washington, DC: CQ, 2012); R.M. Clark, *Intelligence Collection* (Washington, DC: CQ, 2013); M.M. Lowenthal, *Intelligence*; M.M. Lowenthal and R.M. Clark, *The Five Disciplines of Intelligence Collection* (Washington, DC: CQ, 2015); R.J. Heuer, Jr. and R.H. Pherson, *Structured Analytic Techniques for Intelligence Analysis*, 2nd ed. (Washington, DC: CQ, 2014); S.M. Beebe and R.H. Pherson, *Cases in Intelligence Analysis* (Washington, DC: CQ, 2012); also other texts available in the Security and Professional Intelligence Education Series; L. Gearon, 'Education, security and intelligence studies', *British Journal of Educational Studies*, 63, 3 (2015), pp. 263–79; see also articles the *International Journal of Intelligence and Counter-Intelligence*; and *Intelligence and National Security*; L.K. Johnson and M. Phythian, 'Intelligence and national security at thirty', *Journal of Intelligence and National Security*, 31, 1 (2016), pp. 1–7; A.D.M. Svendsen, 'Extending the academy: Advancing functional intelligence studies (FIS)', paper presented at the European Conference of the International Association for Intelligence Education, Netherlands Defence Academy, Breda (22–24 June 2016); A.D.M. Svendsen, 'Teaching an intelligence-based framework for risk', paper presented at the European Conference of the International Association for Intelligence Education, Netherlands Defence Academy, Breda (22–24 June 2016); F. Velasco, 'Editorial', *International Journal of Intelligence, Security, and Public Affairs*, 18, 1 (2016), pp. 1–4.

17. J.H. Ratcliffe, *Intelligence-Led Policing*, 2nd ed. (London: Routledge, 2016), p. 188; for CIA, see F. Konkel, 'Spy chief "excited" about agency's modernization effort', Nextgov.com (25 July 2016).

18. More generally for 'strategic futures' related work, see, e.g., UK Ministry of Defence (MoD), *Global Strategic Trends out to 2045* 5th ed. (Shrivenham, UK: UK Ministry of Defence, 2014); R. Norton-Taylor, 'UK to face growing range of security threats, defence report says', *Guardian* (9 March 2016); 'Strategic Foresight Initiative', Brent Scowcroft Center (2015); U.S. National Intelligence Council, *Global Trends Report* (2015); D. Riechmann, 'Intelligence advice for next president: Rocky road ahead', Associated Press (13 March 2016); D. Blair and R. Sanders, 'Commentary: Preparing the next president for the worst', *Federal Times* (4 August 2016); C. Kojm, 'Global change and megatrends: Implications for intelligence and its oversight', *Lawfare* (12 May 2016); P. Diamandis, 'Robot revolution: These are the breakthroughs you should watch', *SingularityHUB* (15 March 2016); T. O'Reilly, 'Don't replace people. Augment them', *O'Reilly* (20 July 2016); M. Burrows, *The Future, Declassified* (Basingstoke, UK: Palgrave Macmillan, 2014); T. Kasriel, *Futurescaping* (London: Bloomsbury, 2012); C. Coker, 'Rethinking strategy: NATO and the Warsaw Summit', Norwegian Institute of International Affairs (May 2016); A. Sparrow, 'The awful diseases on the way', *New York Times Review of Books* (9 June 2016); H. Pennington, 'Rise of the superbugs', *London Review of Books* (25 May 2016); A. Sifferlin, 'We're fighting zika 'with one hand tied behind our backs', CDC director says', *Time* (26 July 2016); J. Stavridis, 'Zika is just the first front in the 21st-century biowar', *FP* (24 August 2016); M. Weinger, 'Zika: A national security threat?' *The Cipher Brief*; and M. Hardy, 'Mad scientist with a crystal ball: The Army of 2050', *Defense News* (11 August 2016); A. Mehta, 'Joint Force 2035: Lasers, biotech and global instability', *Defense News* (29 July 2016); K. Amerson and S.B. Meredith, III, 'The future operating environment 2050: Chaos, complexity and competition', *Small Wars Journal*; and K. Lilley, 'The millennials have taken over: A primer for the military's generational shift', *Army Times* (31 July 2016); A. Davies, 'The ephemeral offset strategy', *The Strategist* (3 August 2016); D. Sanders, 'Nutrition may be as big a challenge today as HIV/AIDS was 15 years ago', *The Conversation*; M. Tempest, 'Africa's population set to double by 2050, says new report', EurActiv.com; D. Carrington, 'The anthropocene epoch: Scientists declare dawn of human-influenced age', *Guardian*; 'Future of the Arctic: Daunting challenges, big opportunities', *Arctic Journal* (22/29 August 2016).

Chapter One

Introducing Intelligence Engineering

This book briefly introduces and advances the concept of *intelligence engineering* (IE). Embarking on some scene-setting, this chapter (1) comes to a definition covering the landscape as to what IE currently is—or at least presents arguments as to how it might be regarded; (2) presents insights into how IE works—or covers at least how it approximately appears to function; and (3) provides arguments relating to IE's value by answering the questions of *So what?* and *Why should we care?*

Familiar paths are followed. Building on the foundations of the established literature on the themes of intelligence *and* engineering—for instance, as those phenomena are both widely encountered and experienced and, on the whole, are generally and conventionally understood—a broad understanding of more specific IE characteristics is advanced in many of its different observable and far-ranging dimensions.

Much is presented here for continued—and indeed even encouraged—future discussion and debate, including extending beyond the field of intelligence studies. As demonstrated, many different intelligence-related stakeholders, including practitioners, operators to other operatives—including more broadly mainstream business sector and enterprise managers—can capitalise upon IE.

WHAT IS IE?

The definition of IE developed in this book has readily identifiable roots. Recalling the first director general of intelligence at the UK Ministry of Defence (1964–1966) Major-General Sir Kenneth Strong's still-pertinent comment dating from 1968 that 'the initial point of any discussion of Intelligence is of course a definition of the word', this book starts by presenting an updated working definition of 'intelligence'. Particularly, this is as intelligence is manifested in the early twenty-first century—roughly in global terms as it extends across our highly-Westernised world—and into which the relevant engineering facets can then be appropriately integrated.[1]

A Twenty-First-Century Definition of 'Intelligence'

For the purposes of this book, 'intelligence' is defined as

> the collection and processing (analysis) of information that is particularly of military and/or political value, and which especially (and purposefully) relates to international relations, defence and national (extending to global, via regional) security (threats [also encompassing at their most broad, the full-spectrum of 'issues-problems-hazards-to-risks' confronted]). It is also usually secret (covert and/or clandestine), [(and frequently, although not exclusively—as also included are private and sub-/non-state actor contributions)] state activity conducted by specialized 'intelligence' institutions (or organisations) to understand or influence entities.[2]

Dimensions range extensively. Intelligence involves both collection/gathering and analysis/assessment activities, figuring in all-source and multi-INT (different intelligence disciplines) form, spanning across the five spatial physical-to-virtual domains of sea, air, land, space and cyberspace, as well as involving different temporal domains (varying timelines and timeframes). Simultaneously, intelligence consists of (1) higher-level ('big picture') strategic intelligence (STRATINT) and (2) arguably more 'raw' (less-processed or sanitised) and more directly 'actionable', even 'serious', lower-level tactical/operational intelligence (TACINT/OPINT), which is frequently conceptualised as 'military intelligence' (MI, or MILINT), and which is most closely (although not exclusively) associated with the work undertaken by military service (army, air force, navy) intelligence organisations.[3] These overarching definitions of intelligence help to establish a beginning framework and a series of operational parameters for structuring how engineering can be (1) suitably conceptualised and then (2) seen to engage both in intelligence contexts and more specifically with intelligence itself.[4] The phenomenon of IE, essentially rationalised as *most forms of engineering activities figuring in the intelligence context*, then starts to emerge more clearly. Inevitably some caveats apply, featuring later in this book as IE Cautions.[5]

DEFINING 'ENGINEERING'

A more in-depth definition of what is more precisely meant by 'engineering', as it most strongly features in relation to intelligence contexts or the 'intelligence world', is helpful for subsequent analysis. Again, observations and experience show that many different definitions of 'engineering' stand out. However, as is found with 'intelligence'—for instance, as defined above and where constitutively it is a broad and diversely encompassing phenomenon—a similarly broad and diverse definition of 'engineering' emerges as being most satisfactory. This is when the phenomenon of engineering is taken as being most relevant to both intelligence and all of its associated activities and contexts. These areas span operations, jobs, projects, processes, programmes, and missions while extending to all of the 'intelligence dynamics' familiarly involved in intelligence contexts, such as flows of information (information flows) and intelligence coverage-to-reach (with added active influence value attached).[6] The *Oxford English Dictionary* (OED) defines engineering as

1. the branch of science and technology concerned with the design, building, and use of engines, machines, and structures.
   - a field of study or activity concerned with modification or development in a particular area. . . .
2. the action of working artfully to bring something about.[7]

Meanwhile, University of Bristol Engineering Professor David Blockley draws upon his experience to flesh out the above definition by noting that engineering is 'the discipline of using scientific and technical knowledge to imagine, design, create, make, operate, maintain, and dismantle complex devices, machines, structures, systems, and processes that support human endeavour'.[8]

Via both of the above definitions of engineering, and particularly when we are thinking in terms of intelligence, both artistic and scientific, extending to human and technical/technological aspects, are highlighted, together with their greater combination. These definitions now provide us with a helpful springboard from which to further consider how the overall concept of intelligence engineering can be most satisfactorily conceptualised and structured.

A DEFINITION OF INTELLIGENCE ENGINEERING

Collectively drawing on the definitions of both 'intelligence' and 'engineering' presented thus far in this chapter, we can fashion a composite definition of intelligence engineering (IE) out of their fusion. A compelling case can therefore be made for IE as at least roughly constituting in all of its prevailing complexity and diversity

the use of scientific and technical knowledge to artfully bring about (deliver or implement) the design, building, and use of engines, machines, and structures, and equally the study and activity related to the modification or development of those entities, in order to imagine, design, create, make, operate, maintain, and dismantle complex devices, machines, structures, systems, and processes that support and/or disrupt human endeavour occurring both in and/or overlapping with the more specific intelligence context—spanning both human intelligence (HUMINT) and technical intelligence (TECHINT) realms—and which, in turn, significantly involves the collection and processing (analysis) of information that is particularly of military and/or political value, and which especially (and purposefully) relates to international relations, defence, and national (extending to global, via regional) security (threats, encompassing at their most broad, the full-spectrum of issues-problems-hazards-up-to-risks confronted). The last of these efforts frequently also involves secret (covert and/or clandestine), and often (although not exclusively—as private and sub-/non-state actor contributions are also included) state activity conducted by specialized 'intelligence' institutions (or organisations) to understand or influence entities.

Appropriately reflecting the nature of IE, short and easy definitions of IE remain elusive, particularly as we seek an all-encompassing clarity relating to the IE phenomenon while continuing to underscore the importance of the philosophy that the whole is greater than the sum of its individual constitutive parts.

INTRODUCING NEXT DIRECTIONS

Naturally, many further questions now emerge. Drawing heavily on event and development-related questions, concerning the *How? When?* and *Where?* of IE, both in operational to strategic terms, IE articulates the 'ways' and 'means' that we employ during intelligence activities. Equally, IE-related ways and means are again subject to deployment on both an individual and a collective basis. We see this—for instance, as listed above—in operations and other missions so as to achieve overarching and often strategic 'ends', as discussed below.[9]

In the intelligence context, beyond merely strong associations with artificial intelligence (AI)—covered in this book by those AI dimensions encompassed in references to continually-evolving collective intelligence (COLINT) paradigms—perhaps one of the most obvious examples of IE currently in practice or action relates to what is commonly defined as 'social engineering'. As is well-known, many different activities, including those for strategic communication to influence purposes, are included in that definition.[10]

IE VALUE

IE boasts many operational and strategic ways, means, and ends. Similar to multiple systems and management-to-business enterprise-laden intelligence, surveillance, (target acquisition), and reconnaissance or IS(TA)R work—which is frequently combined with command, control, communications, and computers (C4) concerns to generate C4ISR efforts—IE activities allow for greater fusion, connection, and feedback-looping interaction between military-headquarters-related #2 Intelligence (e.g., G/J2) and #3 Operations (e.g., G/J3) domains of activity. Similarly included are civilian activities involving civil-military (CIV/MIL) and political-military (POL/MIL) concepts. In turn, these efforts are embedded in an overarching strategic context focused on, for example, overall task, job, and mission accomplishment ends.[11] In sum, IE encompasses (1) intelligence-associated collection/gathering and analysis/assessment (estimate) work to (2) the further operationalised implementation of plans and intents generated by commanders and other high-level leaders and policy- to decision-makers. In current circumstances, several 'edges' benefit from their 'extra sharpening' to gain advantage.[12]

In 2016, as: (1) the Islamic State (IS) - also known as the Islamic State of Iraq and al-Sham or Syria (ISIS), the Islamic State of Iraq and the Levant (ISIL), and Da'esh—continues to increasingly crystallise as the number 1 target and threat for several intelligence agencies located in many different countries and regions across the world;[13] as (2) hybrid defence or, at least, substantially destabilising 'ground-to-bottom-up' warfare concepts gain traction in areas such as Ukraine and across other contested and escalating battlespaces that span physical to virtual sea, air, land, space and cyberspace geostrategic domains, while simultaneously being influenced by 'glocalisation' (often messy global-local combinations), and covering operational-to-strategy-related ways, means, and ends;[14] and as (3) key intelligence themes figure, including intelligence liaison extending to its professionalisation as well as the nationalisation, regionalisation, and globalisation of intelligence, which overlap at times with what can be paradoxical and even contradictory internationalisation, centralisation, fragmentation, atomisation and nodalisation trends—all emerge as increasingly important processes and mechanisms on which to maintain close focus through their further in-depth study and greater understanding.[15]

Contemporary concerns, such as the—at least perceived—erosion of European to global security, are truly 'multiplexic', reflecting conditions and situations of 'multiplexity'.[16] They firmly demonstrate where IE again has a significant role to articulate as well as emphasising the value IE can bring to overall defence and security enterprises.

THE 'INTELLIGENCE *AND* LAW' NEXUS

Neglecting developments and embedding contexts that occur more widely would be amiss. Hand-in-glove most notably around the years 2014–2016, the 'intelligence *and* law' theme has undergone some revolution.[17] The changes relate especially to 'big data'–type, large-scale or large-sample-size (large-*N*)—often claimed to be 'bulk' or 'mass'—surveillance and closely associated issues, such as metadata use, encryption, and so-called backdoor access. These are all hard-pressed in the post–Snowden affected intelligence world. As suggested above, these developments, not always for the better and auguring a more challenging future for intelligence, require continued adjustment for several different participants.[18] Notably:

> When dealing with distributed Big Data, developments and events . . . as well as their associated patterns, '4Vs' standout. These include the 'quantitative considerations' of: (i) *'Volume'* (e.g., 'scale/size of data/developments and events'); and (ii) *'Velocity'* ('analysis of streaming/flows of data/developments and events'); as well as evaluating the 'qualitative factors' of: (iii) *'Variety'* ('differentiated forms of data/developments and events'); and [(arguably with most relevance with regard to intelligence work)] (iv) *'Veracity'* ('uncertainty of and relating to data/developments and events').[19]

Collectively, both qualitatively and quantitatively, some positive and—those mitigations aside—severely less-helpful and more negatively ranging dimensions, are all upheld. As 'hard law', 'legalisation', and 'legalism' trends become more pronounced in investigative contexts, intelligence work does not escape unscathed. It requires at least some extended defence to keep at least some channels and necessary opportunities and possibilities open and adequately in play. Intelligence-related 'tips' and 'leads' continue to require sufficient scope or flexible room for manoeuvre if they are to be followed up most advantageously. This applies even if that work is more explorative and is occurring more experimentally. Moreover, intelligence is not and should never be taken as, or be confused and merged or muddled with, evidence. There are distinct, qualitative differences between them, as their different definitions and functions strongly suggest.[20]

Here is another area where IE and its closely associated concepts perform an important role. Across the board of the 'intelligence *and* law' landscapes just described, more appropriate—indeed, 'smarter'— balances are required. The much-challenged surveillance law–related changes seen to date have been most notable in the United States and in many other prominent Western capitals such as London, Berlin, and Paris, together with being witnessed at the European Union (EU) level. Partly following characteristic incremental-movement trends, we can anticipate further changes in surveillance systems to oversight and accountability mechanisms in the form of 'on-going issue-management' approaches.[21] IE can help design and guide these subsequent moves.

IE AS NAVIGATOR AND NEGOTIATOR

Indeed, IE offers us a viable roadmap. Demanding much continued education and enhanced technical-to-technological prowess, the above-noted status of constant change and associated disruption prevails because an overarching consensus is lacking and the challenges encountered remain very much in flux on widespread bases. For instance, multiple, far-ranging 'big' questions soon follow requiring us to find more sophisticated intelligence-related metrics and more enhanced, both qualitative and quantitative, performance indicators. For example, 'What is "mass" and "bulk" surveillance, and how effective is it?' and 'Is "looking at" and "exploring" or "handling" data—for instance, for pattern discovery—the same as "reading" and "examining" content?' 'What, where, and how should "legal parameters" exist?' 'What does this mean for grander concepts such as "privacy", "security", "safety", "secrecy", "liberty", and "luxury"?' 'What are the differences between "data", "information", "intelligence", "knowledge", and "wisdom"?' 'Do we prefer "horizontal" ("skimming the surface/scanning the horizon") or "vertical" ("delving deeper/more invasive") surveillance regimes?' and 'Can we cope with activity occurring more hidden away on—qualitatively different—social media, in the Cloud, and on the Deep Web and the Dark Web or the "Darknet", as well as involving the rapidly evolving Internet of Things (IoT)?'[22] Of course, there are no easy answers to any of these questions, and most valid and enduring mitigations will take time to be formulated.

Together with other generalisations, overall balances remain ambiguous. The fashioning of many protective 'buffer-zones' is advantageous. These feature as appropriately negotiated 'safeguards'—for instance, adopting *privacy-by-design* approaches, including conducting privacy impact assessments (PIAs)—which increasingly figure in intelligence-related endeavours. They also appear as the 'least-worst-case' compromises, or 'lesser evils', that strive to be realised then maintained in overall governance contexts as well as in other enterprises.[23] What is clear is that overly vague or opaque definitions of key terms contained within legislation or in analyses are instead much more unhelpful. Expansion requires careful control, especially when IE is involved.[24]

Although they are difficult to grasp in their sheer totality, the slew of problematic issues in the area of 'intelligence *and* law' go beyond solely government and public sectors. With 'data intelligence' (DATINT) and its handling remaining central, the challenges encountered also substantially reach into private, commercial and business realms, as global technology companies such as Twitter, Facebook, Apple and Alphabet (Google) can especially attest.[25] A highly complex picture therefore remains, and it is one that continues to elude simple and easy characterisation in its plurality of systematic and systemic effects and outcomes. A whole range of complications endure as offshoots ripple out, simultaneously cascading in several directions over various time zones and across many different locations worldwide, and as they all occur at varying rates of manifestation (in terms of momentum and so forth).[26]

IE AS AN AID IN ADDRESSING PERSISTENT CHALLENGES

An occasionally loud and immature to naïve dissatisfaction currently reigns, and is expected to continue for some time into the future.[27] We see that (1) 'collective security' or 'public safety' and 'responsibility to protect, even prevent (R2P)' concerns, versus/vis-à-vis (2) 'individual privacy' consider-ations, versus/vis-à-vis (3) the 'tech industry' (its vitality, economic viability, competitiveness, and so forth) dynamics all exist and at the same time. Once more, no easy or simple solutions are available.

However, IE offers help. Amid these many prevailing conditions of dissent and even almost toxic dispute, we have to realise effective navigation and balancing. This work involves at least attempts toward reconciliation, moving more from oppositional conditions of *versus* to those more cooperative, even complementary, conditions of *vis-à-vis*, as far as is possible.[28] Importantly, law is not immune to or incompatible with engineering and its closely associ-ated tasks, which points to further degrees of accommodation and flexibility. Creative, 'smarter' ways forward remain viable and have potential for being seized.[29] Greater contextualisation fashioned through progressive IE efforts remains of widespread benefit.

Ultimately, when we confront all the challenges outlined above, the utility of IE becomes increasingly apparent. For its many different stakeholders, IE offers a toolbox with a variety of toolsets, a veritable equipment smorgas-bord, ready for use in various ways and requiring judicious application.[30] Selecting the right, or at least most appropriate, tool for each IE-related task is necessary. Otherwise, naturally, given the sensitive domains being negoti-ated, we can easily expect negative repercussions. This is especially the case if the requisite, baseline 'know-how' of specific contextual or more technical understanding is missing through its absence or whether it is rather neglected or even ignored.[31]

THE TERRAIN COVERED BY THIS BOOK

After beginning with the origins of IE, chapter 2 goes on to briefly survey recent key literature relating to 'intelligence as "art" and "science"'. Rather than merely repeating at length well-worn debates on the theme, the aim of the chapter is to draw out the core aspects of the prevailing discussion that emerge as being most relevant to this book's more specific focus on IE. Chapter 2 then continues by further sketching the intelligence-engineering relationship by exploring how different engineering dimensions relate to intelligence.

In chapter 3, discussion moves to how we get from #2 Intelligence to #3 Operations, and back, via facets such as System of Systems Dynamics (SoSD). On the way, chapter 3 further examines the military headquarters–related G/J2 Intelligence and G/J3 Operations domains and introduces levels, systems, and SoSD in all of their observable detail. This evaluation includes both System of Systems Analysis (SoSA) and System of Systems Engineering (SoSE) dimensions, and how and where they are harnessed—whether well or not—in contemporary intelligence-related contexts. Acting also as a facilitator—and by advocating the adoption of much more of a full-spectrum-ranging theme-issue-problem-hazard-risk up and across to threat-orientated approach in terms of recommended focussing, targeting, prioritisation, and then addressing-to-solving—IE helps glue that above important lengthy list of interconnected activities into more of a coherent whole.

Directly following on this discussion, chapter 4 focuses on advancing what is called 'an IE-based framework for risk'. That framework is relevant to risk analysis and risk assessment for better understanding the uncertainty we are experiencing now in current circumstances and the uncertainty anticipated in the future. Chapter 4 includes communicating the potential for that framework to be applied in subsequent risk management efforts. Both a priori and post facto concerns and considerations feature. There is a strong focus on positioning, such as getting 'ahead of'—while simultaneously generating an improved awareness that we might instead be more 'behind'—event and development 'curves' as they unfold, at times rapidly.

Chapter 5 presents conclusions relating to IE and possible dangers. Showing where distinct IE caveats exist, chapter 5 especially emphasises that IE, particularly as it is introduced and conceptualised throughout this book, is not the same as 'engineering intelligence' or the 'engineering *of* intelligence'. Those last approaches and methodologies can have more dangerous consequences and wider negative ramifications. These are 'blowback' reminders, dimensions that history has shown are worth watching closely and carefully, while astutely avoiding blowback. More than enough 'misfortune' already abounds as it is with regard to intelligence and its associated work.[32] Finally, chapter 5 offers some answers to the question of *Where next?* for the future of IE.

NOTES

1. See, e.g., Strong as cited in A.D.M. Svendsen, *Understanding the Globalization of Intelligence* (Basingstoke, UK: Palgrave Macmillan, 2012), p. 3; A.D.M. Svendsen, '1968—"A year to remember" for the study of British intelligence?' in C.R. Moran and C.J. Murphy, eds., *Intelligence Studies in Britain and the US* (Edinburgh: Edinburgh University Press, 2013).

2. Svendsen, *Understanding the Globalization of Intelligence*, pp. 9–10; see also the definition in A.D.M. Svendsen, 'Making arms control "smarter"? The importance of intelligence', *Utrikes Perspektiv* (2015), p. 56; for further useful definitions of 'intelligence', see e.g., M.M. Lowenthal, *Intelligence* (Washington, DC: CQ Press, 2015 [6 ed.]); inter alia, R.Z. George, 'Intelligence and strategy', chapter 8 in J. Baylis et al., eds., *Strategy in the Contemporary World* (Oxford: Oxford University Press, 2016 [5 ed.]); M.I. Handel, 'Deception, surprise, and intelligence', chapter 15 in *Masters of War* (London: Routledge, 2001 [3 ed.]); references to intelligence in J. Ångström and J.J. Widén, *Contemporary Military Theory* (London: Routledge, 2015); B.J. Sutherland, ed., *Modern Warfare, Intelligence and Deterrence* (London: Economist/Wiley, 2011). For other official, contemporary, and functional definitions of 'intelligence', e.g., via 'JCAT releases 2016 intelligence guide for first responders', *Information Sharing Environment—ISE Bulletin* (14 March 2016).

3. See, e.g., as summarised in A.D.M. Svendsen, 'Intelligence, surveillance and reconnaissance (ISR)', in J. Deni and D. Galbreath, eds., *The Routledge Handbook of Defence Studies* (London: Routledge, forthcoming); see also A.D.M. Svendsen, *Intelligence Cooperation and the War on Terror* (London: Routledge, 2010), pp. 41–42; B. Wittes, 'Heritage foundation conference on "The role of intelligence" video', *Lawfare* (3 April 2016); K. Brannen, 'Spies-for-hire now at war in Syria', *The Daily Beast* (8 August 2016); S. Clark, 'China: The new space superpower', *Guardian* (29 August 2016).

4. See also A.D.M. Svendsen, 'The Globalization of intelligence since 9/11: Frameworks and operational parameters', *Cambridge Review of International Affairs*, 21, 1 (March 2008), pp. 129–44; C. Bing, 'New intelligence program aims to stop supply chain Hacks', *FedScoop* (11 August 2016).

5. See, for instance, as discussed further in chapter 5 of this book.

6. On 'intelligence dynamics', Svendsen, *Understanding the Globalization of Intelligence*, p. 235; A.D.M. Svendsen, *The Professionalization of Intelligence Cooperation* (Basingstoke, UK: Palgrave Macmillan, 2012), p. 241; A.D.M. Svendsen, 'Contemporary intelligence innovation in practice', *Defence Studies*, 15, 2 (2015), esp. pp. 108–9; C.F. Jackson, 'Information is not a weapons system', *Journal of Strategic Studies* (7 March 2016).

7. 'Engineering' definition from the *Oxford Dictionary of English* (2015).

8. D. Blockley, *Engineering* (Oxford: Oxford University Press, 2012), p. xi.

9. For this conceptualisation and structuring of strategic approaches, see, e.g., D.S. Reveron and J.L. Cook, 'From national to theater: Developing strategy', *Joint Forces Quarterly*, 70 (2013), pp. 113–20.

10. Svendsen, *The Professionalization of Intelligence Cooperation*, p. 155, as well as discussed at least partially further later throughout this study; see also A.D.M. Svendsen, 'Re-fashioning risk', *Defence Studies*, 10, 3 (September 2010), pp. 307–35; I. Cobain, A. Ross, R. Evans, and M. Mahmood, 'Revealed: UK's covert propaganda bid to stop Muslims joining ISIS', *Guardian*; and S. Salaheddin and S. George, 'US struggles to convince Iraqis it doesn't support IS', Associated Press (2/8 May 2016); 'DNA databases deter crime, without filling prisons', *Brookings*, S. Yom and K. Sammour, 'The social terrain of Islamist radicalization: Insights from Jordan', *Lawfare*; and 'Islamist extremists to be held in special prison units', BBC (16/21/22 August 2016); H.J. Ingram, 'An analysis of *Inspire* and *Dabiq*: Lessons from AQAP and Islamic State's propaganda war', *Studies in Conflict and Terrorism* (July 2016); J.P. Farwell, 'Victory in today's wars: New insights on the role of communications', *Parameters*, 46, 2 (2016), pp. 93–100; D. Paul, 'Pen-test trio crafts "datasploit" tool for easy social engineering', *Register*; and J. Detsch, 'Can hackers sway public opinion with DNC and NSA leaks?' *Christian Science Monitor* (15/22 August 2016); T.P. Gerber and J. Zavisca, 'Does Russian propaganda work?' *Washington Quarterly*, 39, 2 (2016), pp. 79–98; N. MacFarquhar, 'A powerful Russian weapon: The spread of false stories', *New York Times* (29 August 2016); see also the 'artificial intelligence' (AI) and 'computer science' references in A.D.M. Svendsen, 'Collective intelligence (COLINT)' in G. Moore, ed., *Encyclopedia of U.S. Intelligence* (New York: CRC Press, 2014); T.W. Malone and M.S. Bernstein, eds., *Handbook of Collective Intelligence* (Cambridge, MA: MIT Press, 2015); S. Russell and P. Norvig, *Artificial Intelligence* (Harlow, UK: Pearson, 2016 [3rd ed.]); 'Artificial intelligence: Google's AlphaGo beats go master Lee Se-dol', BBC (12 March 2016); M. Pomerleau, 'Pentagon research chief: AI is powerful but has critical limitations', *Defense Systems*; and T. O'Reilly, 'Why AI is finally going mainstream', *O'Reilly*; N. Alang, 'Who's afraid of artificial intelligence?' *New Republic*; and J. Guszcza and N. Maddirala, 'Minds and machines: The art of forecasting in the age of artificial intelligence', *Deloittes* (4/24/26 May/25 July 2016); N. Bhuta et al., eds., *Autonomous Weapons Systems* (Cambridge: Cambridge University Press, 2016); M. Zenko, '"Autonomy": A smart overview of the Pentagon's robotic plans', *CFR*; and P. Tucker, 'DOD Science Board recommends "immediate action" to counter enemy AI', *Defense One* (23/25 August 2016).

11. Svendsen, *The Professionalization of Intelligence Cooperation*, p. 6, pp. 17–18, p. 112, p. 144; R. Thakur, 'The responsibility to protect at 15', *International Affairs*, 92 (2016), pp. 415–34.

12. Svendsen, *The Professionalization of Intelligence Cooperation*, esp., p. 17; A.D.M. Svendsen, 'Advancing "defence-in-depth"', *Defense & Security Analysis*, 31, 1, (2015), p. 60 and p. 67; M.V. Hayden, *Playing to the Edge* (New York: Penguin, 2016); D. Ignatius, 'America is no longer guaranteed military victory: these weapons could change that', *Washington Post* (16 August 2016); B. Opall-Rome, 'A cautionary tale of the Israel defense forces', *Defense News* (12 August 2016); A.D.M. Svendsen, 'Strategy and disproportionality in contemporary conflicts', *Journal of Strategic Studies*, 33, 3 (June 2010).

13. See as argued in, e.g., A.D.M. Svendsen, 'Developing international intelligence liaison against Islamic State: Approaching 'one for all and all for one'?' *International Journal of Intelligence and CounterIntelligence*, 29, 2 (2016); J. Gould, 'Dunford: Better intel improving counter-ISIS airstrikes', *Defense News* (29 March 2016); P. Stewart, 'U.S. says it, allies to do more to combat Islamic State', Reuters (4 May 2016); D. Butler and V. Ghirda, 'Nuclear black market seeks IS extremists', Associated Press (7 October 2015); J. Warrick, *Black Flags* (London: Bantam, 2015); S. Salaheddin, 'Iraq defends intelligence sharing with Russia, Syria, Iran', Associated Press (28 September 2015); 'Libya IS head "Killed in US air strike"', and 'How Jihadi John was tracked down in Syria', BBC (14 November 2015); P. Parameswaran, 'Malaysia to host new conference to tackle Islamic State challenge', *Diplomat* (8 October 2015); D. Gartenstein-Ross and N. Barr, 'Neither remaining nor expanding: The Islamic State's global expansion struggles', *War on the Rocks* (23 February 2016); 'Confronting failed government and the Islamic State in Libya', *International Institute for Strategic Studies Strategic Comments*, 22, 1 (February 2016); 'Targeting the Islamic State in Libya', Soufan Group (2 August 2016); V. Dodd, 'ISIS planning "Enormous and spectacular attacks", anti-terror chief warns', *Guardian*; 'Foreign fighters and those who return', Soufan Group; P. Rogers, 'The extending war: ISIS to AQIM', *Open Democracy*; and J. Burke, 'The tyranny of ISIS terrorism will not always be with us, but history shows that a new militant threat will emerge', *Guardian* (7/9/18/27 March 2016); H. Yan, 'Not just ISIS: terror groups worldwide jockey for power', CNN (4 August 2016); 'After Brussels: Understanding and countering ISIS's strategy', *International Institute for Strategic Studies Strategic Comments* (30 March 2016); 'Arrests in Denmark indicate likely use of leaked Islamic State documents by European intelligence agencies', IHS Jane's 360; 'German intelligence head admits "Misjudgment" on 'Islamic State' strategy', *Deutsche Welle*; and N. Mousavizadeh, 'Islamic State has erased the line between foreign and domestic policy', Reuters (7/10/21 April 2016); J. McLaughlin, 'The Islamic State: Dangerous like a wounded beast', Ozy; L. Sly, 'The war against the Islamic State hits hurdles just as the U.S. military gears up', *Washington Post*; and E. Schmitt, 'U.S. says its strikes are hitting more significant ISIS targets', *New York Times* (6/8/25 May 2016); I. Ali and W. Strobel, 'Kerry calls for new measures to counter changing Islamic State', Reuters; and E. Schmitt, 'U.S. secures vast new trove of intelligence on ISIS', *New York Times* (21/27 July 2016); 'Afghan official says major offensive against ISIS underway', Associated Press; B. Seftel, 'The ISIS-Al Qaeda rivalry', *Time*; and 'A diaspora of terror', Soufan Group (26/28 July 2016); T. Joscelyn, 'Jihadists argue over leadership of Islamic State's West Africa province', *Long War Journal*; A. Tilghman, 'Top U.S. commander in Iraq says Islamic State group will "morph into a true insurgent force"', *Military Times*; and M. Ryan, 'New commander will increase tempo of U.S. operations in conclusive stage of ISIS fight', *Washington Post* (4/10/21 August 2016); L. Morris, 'Islamic State, losing fighters and territory, increasingly turns to child bombers', *Washington Post*; A. Liepman and C.P. Clarke, 'Demystifying the Islamic State', Rand Corporation; and 'Zawahri urges Iraq Sunnis to wage guerrilla war as IS loses more land', Reuters (22/23/25 August 2016); J. Steele, 'At least 1,500 Iranians prevented from joining IS: Intelligence minister', *Middle East Eye*; and

'Islamic State "connected" to Bangladesh, says Kerry, offering security aid', Reuters (26/29 August 2016).

14. See, inter alia, M. Galeotti, 'Time to think about "hybrid defense"', *War on the Rocks* (30 July 2015); A.D.M. Svendsen, 'Strategic futures and intelligence: The head and heart of "hybrid defence" providing tangible meaning and ways forward' (draft article); E. Simpson, *War From the Ground Up* (London: Hurst, 2012); R. Smith, *The Utility of Force* (London: Penguin, 2006); I. Goldenberg and N.A. Heras, 'Securing Syria region-by-region from the bottom up', *Defense One* (25 February 2016); R. Kheel, 'Top US commander: Russia wants to "rewrite" international order', *The Hill*; 'NATO commander: Russia poses "existential threat" to West', and E. Tomiuc, 'EU discord deepens amid warnings of looming "humanitarian crisis"', Radio Free Europe/ Radio Liberty (25 February 2016); D.A. Ollivant, 'The rise of the hybrid warriors: From Ukraine to the Middle East', *War on the Rocks* (9 March 2016); 'Urgent steps needed towards full respect for ceasefire in Eastern Ukraine, says OSCE', BBC (28 July 2016); A. Osborn, 'Russia announces war games after accusing Ukraine of terrorist plot', 'Ukraine could introduce martial law if eastern fighting worsens—Poroshenko', and 'Kremlin says Putin, Merkel, Hollande to meet to discuss Ukraine at G20 on Sept. 4–5', Reuters (11/18/23 August 2016); D. Jordan et al., *Understanding Modern Warfare* (Cambridge: Cambridge University Press, 2016 [2 ed.]), pp. 8–9.

15. See also Svendsen, *The Professionalization of Intelligence Cooperation*; A.D.M. Svendsen, 'Intelligence liaison', *Intelligencer*—AFIO (May 2015); Svendsen, 'International intelligence liaison: A primer'; J. van Buuren, 'From oversight to undersight: The internationalization of intelligence', *Security and Human Rights Blog* (2014), esp. p. 241; A. Panda, 'India and Pakistan are set to join the Shanghai Cooperation Organization: So what?' *Diplomat* (7 July 2015); 'German spy says Salafists trying to recruit refugees—Newspaper', Reuters; and S. Mekhennet and W. Booth, 'Migrants are disguising themselves as Syrians to enter Europe', *Washington Post* (18/23 September 2015); D. Wasserbly, 'DoD, intelligence community establishing joint space centre', IHS Jane's 360; L.K. Bate, 'In search of cyber deterrence', *War on the Rocks*; N. Mousavizadeh, 'The weaponization of everything: Globalization's dark side', Reuters; and 'Regional organizations central to global efforts in countering violent Extremism', Organization for Security and Co-operation in Europe (14/24–25/29 September 2015); 'Saudi Arabia's escalating fight with Iran', Soufan Group (7 March 2016); P. Welsh, 'Improving searches for intel information', *USAF Materiel Command News* (15 April 2016); M. Hosenball, 'Spy agencies struggle to spot threats from lone, mentally ill attackers', Reuters (23 July 2016); M. Carter, 'Illinois moves toward advancing a distributed and decentralized information sharing environment', 'Wanted by the FBI: Agencies that report crime data via NIBRS', 'NESPIN welcomes Connecticut Intelligence Center (CTIC) to group of agency systems connected to RISSNET', and 'ISE reports accomplishments, identifies goals in 2016 annual report', *ISE Bulletin* (26 July–August 2016); W. Young and D. Stebbins, 'A rapidly changing urban environment', Rand Corporation (2016); D. Kilcullen, *Out of the Mountains* (London: Hurst, 2013).

16. For further discussion and definition of this concept, see chapter 3; J. Andrews, *The World in Conflict* (London: Economist, 2015); M. Pomerleau, 'Info-sharing

hurdles hinders alliance partnerships', C4ISRNet; S. Brill, '15 years after 9/11, is America any safer?' *Defense One*; 'Italy, Germany, France Eye beefed up EU defense after recent terror attacks', Associated Press; 'Europeans turn to weapons in growing numbers after attacks', Reuters (8/11/22/23 August 2016).

17. For earlier 'intelligence and law' insights, see esp. 'The legal dimension' in Svendsen, *The Professionalization of Intelligence Cooperation*, from p. 23, also via p. 241, col. 2; see also 'The legal dimension gathers momentum' in Svendsen, *Understanding the Globalization of Intelligence*, from p. 30, also p. 8, and via p. 236 col. 2.

18. For background, see, e.g., D. Lyon, *Surveillance Studies* (Cambridge: Polity, 2007); S. Chesterman, 'Privacy and surveillance in the age of terror', *Survival*, 52, 5 (2010), pp. 31–46; and S. Chesterman, *One Nation under Surveillance* (Oxford: Oxford University Press, 2011); S. Landau, *Surveillance or Security?* (Cambridge, MA: MIT Press, 2011); for further context, see, e.g., V. Mayer-Schönberger and K. Cukier, *Big Data* (London: John Murray, 2013); and V. Mayer-Schönberger and K. Cukier, 'The rise of big data', *Foreign Affairs* (May/June 2013); C.L. Borgman, *Big Data, Little Data, No Data* (Cambridge, MA: MIT Press, 2015); A. Bunnik et al. (eds.), *Big Data Challenges* (Basingstoke, UK: Palgrave Macmillan, 2016); W. Hayes, 'The dark side of big data', *Forbes* (14 September 2015); P.B. Symon and A. Tarapore, 'Defense intelligence analysis in the age of big data', *Joint Forces Quarterly*, 79 (2015), pp. 4–11; C. Pham, 'Effectiveness of metadata information and tools applied to national security', *Library Philosophy and Practice*, Paper 1077 (2014); D. Lowe, 'Surveillance and international terrorism intelligence exchange', *Terrorism and Political Violence* (August 2014); J. Pomerantz, *Metadata* (Cambridge, MA: MIT Press, 2015); O. Kerr, 'Relative vs. absolute approaches to the content/metadata line', *Lawfare* (25 August 2016); A.J. Martin, 'PGP Zimmerman: "You want privacy? Well privacy costs money"', *Register* (8 October 2015); P. Rosenzweig, 'How concerned should we be about IoT vulnerability?' *Lawfare* (12 February 2016); M. Carollo, 'Most encryption products far beyond reach of US law enforcement', *Christian Science Monitor*; M. Burgess, 'UK court: GCHQ hacking phones and computers is legal', *Wired*; and C. Savage, 'N.S.A. gets less web data than believed, report suggests', *New York Times* (February 2016); J. Hattem, 'NSA "not interested in" Americans, privacy officer claims', 'Lawmakers warn of "radical" move by NSA to share information', *The Hill*; G. Friedman, 'Fighting terrorism requires massive intrusion into Society', EurActiv.com; and D. Kravets, 'FBI director says fight with Apple about terrorism, not setting precedent', *ArsTechnica* (March 2016); G. Corera, 'The spies of tomorrow will need to love data', *Wired*; and K.G. Coleman, 'Drowning in data', C4ISRNet (7/11 April 2016); P. Tran, 'Border security based on data mining', *Defense News*, C. Vallance, 'Spies "staggering" data requests revealed', BBC; and O. Bowcott and R. Norton-Taylor, 'UK spy agencies have collected bulk personal data since 1990s, files show', *Guardian* (9/21 April 2016); K.B. Williams, 'Twitter bars intelligence agencies from key data service', *The Hill*; and S. Dinan, 'Government still holding on to 5 years of NSA phone-snooping metadata', *Washington Times* (9/27 May 2016); J. Daskal and A.K. Woods, 'Congress should embrace the DOJ's cross-Border data fix', *Lawfare* (1 August 2016); K. Waddell, 'Did the NSA get hacked?' *Atlantic*, N. Weaver, 'NSA and the no good, very bad Monday', *Lawfare*, J. Vijayan, 'NSA leak

rattles cybersecurity industry', *Christian Science Monitor*; and 'US intelligence still sorting out purported NSA hack', Associated Press (16/20/24 August 2016); 'Britain needs bulk data interception for security, review says', Reuters (19 August 2016); see also other relevant and related sources cited throughout this chapter.

19. Svendsen, 'Intelligence, surveillance and reconnaissance (ISR)'; Symon and Tarapore, 'Defense intelligence analysis in the age of big data'; C. Meserole, 'National security in a data age', *Lawfare* (5 June 2016); A. Boyd, 'DoDIIS16 takeaway: Spy gadgets aren't about exploding cigarettes anymore', C4ISRNet; J. Baker, 'Germany eyes facial recognition tech for airports, train stations', *ArsTechnica*; and M. Peck, 'Air Force wants more TID-BIT', C4ISRNet (4/22/29 August 2016).

20. See, e.g., A.D.M. Svendsen, '"Smart Law" for intelligence!', *Tech & Law Center* (Milan University, Italy: June 2015); E.A. Posner, *The Perils of Global Legalism* (Chicago: University of Chicago Press, 2009); C. Inglis and J. Kosseff, 'In defense of FAA Section 702', *Lawfare* (29 April 2016). For UK developments, notably: D. Anderson, *A Question of Trust: Report of the Investigatory Powers Review* (June 2015); 'UK surveillance 'lacks transparency', ISC report says', BBC (12 March 2015); 'Independent Surveillance Review publishes report: "A democratic licence to operate"', *RUSI* (14 July 2015); 'UK spying law would undermine tech industry, MPs warn', and P. Strasburger, 'Snooping law must be 'fundamentally rethought and rebuilt', Lord Strasburger says', *Wired* (1/11 February 2016); A. Travis, 'Snoopers' charter: Wider police powers to hack phones and access web history', *Guardian*; and 'Surveillance law: Revised bill adds privacy safeguards', BBC (2 March 2016); R. Mason and A. Travis, 'Snooper's charter: Lib Dems accuse Labour of 'sitting on their hands''', *Guardian*; D. Severson, 'Taking stock of the snoopers' charter: The U.K.'s Investigatory Powers Bill', *Lawfare*; R. Mason, A. Asthana, and A. Travis, '"Snooper's charter": Theresa May faces calls to improve bill to protect privacy'''; 'Investigatory Powers Bill: May defends surveillance powers', BBC; and K. McCann, '"Snoopers' charter": Government wins vote on Investigatory Powers Bill', *Daily Telegraph* (14–15 March 2016); 'British MPs pass new digital surveillance law', Reuters; and M.J. Schwartz, 'Brexit: What's next for privacy, policing, surveillance?' Information Security Media Group (7/29 June 2016); 'UK Royal Society's #1 cybersecurity recommendation: Don't backdoor crypto', *BoingBoing*; and M. Weaver, 'MI5 resisting independent oversight of bulk data collection', *Guardian* (18/26 July 2016); 'Internet spying powers backed by review', BBC; S. Khan, 'Terror attack on Britain foiled 'in its final hours', report says', *Guardian*; P. Norris, 'Revealed: How GCHQ helped foil terror plot against UK hours before attack and freed hostages', *Gloucestershire Live* (19–21 August 2016); 'France, Germany press for access to encrypted messages after attacks', Reuters (23 August 2016).

21. See, e.g., R. Brand, 'What does effective intelligence oversight look like?'; J. Harman, 'Why intelligence oversight matters: Congress is key to a public debate', *Lawfare* (3/13 May 2016); J. Hattem, 'House eyes new chance to reform surveillance', *The Hill* (15 June 2016); see also R. Litt, 'Opinion: Europe's court should know the truth about US intelligence', *Financial Times*; and J. Fioretti, 'Europe-U.S. data transfer deal used by thousands of firms is ruled invalid', Reuters (5/7 October 2015); C. Stupp, 'Commission replaces Safe Harbour with rebranded 'privacy

shield'", EurActiv.com; K. Propp, 'Cracks in the ice: US–EU privacy relations start to thaw', *Lawfare*; J. Detsch and C. Maza, 'What to expect from privacy shield', *Christian Science Monitor* (3/18/26 February 2016); C. Barbière, 'MEPs refuse to vote on PNR before council strengthens data protection', EurActiv.com (8 March 2016); K.B. Williams, 'Tech groups hit back at EU privacy regulators', *The Hill*; J. Fioretti, 'U.S. reluctant to change data pact after EU watchdogs' concerns', Reuters; and M. Scott, 'Obama stresses need to monitor data in fighting terrorism', *New York Times* (13/20/25 April 2016); J. Hattem, 'NSA provided key to finding Paris attack suspect', *The Hill* (22 August 2016); J. Baker, 'Privacy Shield faces another setback after Eurocrats fail to agree on deal', *ArsTechnica*; K.B. Williams, 'Facebook case calls transatlantic data transfers into question', *The Hill* (20/25 May 2016); K. Propp, 'Needles in haystacks: The coming threat to trans-Atlantic data transfer agreements', *Lawfare*; A.J. Martin, 'US plans intervention in EU vs Facebook case caused by NSA snooping', *Register*; J. Uchill, 'US seeks to intervene in European privacy case against Facebook', *The Hill*; 'Privacy Shield: White House makes EU spying promise', BBC (8/13/27 June 2016); C. Stupp, 'Privacy Shield agreement signed off despite vote abstentions', 'Privacy Shield forced US to be 'transparent' about intelligence agencies', EurActiv.com; J. Fioretti, 'EU privacy watchdogs keep open mind on new U.S. data pact', Reuters (8/12/26 July 2016); Z.K. Goldman and S.J. Rascoff, eds., *Global Intelligence Oversight* (Oxford: Oxford University Press, 2016); S. Richardson and N. Gilmour, *Intelligence and Security Oversight* (Basingstoke, UK: Palgrave Macmillan, 2016). On 'incrementalism', Svendsen, *Understanding the Globalization of Intelligence*, p. 44, p. 81, p. 91, p. 122; Svendsen, *Intelligence Cooperation and the War on Terror*, p. 63, p. 71, p. 172.

22. See, e.g., M. Glenny, *Dark Market* (London: Bodley Head, 2011); J. Bartlett, *The Dark Net* (London: Windmill, 2014); J. Mullin, 'Silk Road mastermind Ross Ulbricht sentenced to life in prison', *ArsTechnica* (29 May 2015); J. Bearman, 'The untold story of Silk Road—Parts 1&2', *Wired* (April 2015); N. Raymond, 'Key player in Silk Road successor site gets eight years in U.S. prison', Reuters (4 June 2016); 'Hacker advertises details of 117 million LinkedIn users on Darknet', *Guardian* (18 May 2016); 'Merkel defends refugee policy, vows action on "Darknet" after terror attacks', EurActiv.com (29 July 2016); M. Barlow and G. Fell, *Patrolling the Dark Net* (London: O'Reilly, 2016); S. Greengard, *The Internet of Things* (Cambridge, MA: MIT Press, 2015); R. Dooley, 'Small data: The next big thing', and M. Kavis, 'Forget big data—Small data is driving the internet of things', *Forbes* (16/25 February 2016); D. McCabe, 'Consumer protection agency to look at disclosure issues', *The Hill* (24 May 2016); L. Penn-Hall, 'The Clash over social media data', M. Hayden, 'A bad decision', and R. Siers, 'Choose your battles wisely', *Cipher Brief* (24 July 2016); J. Karsten, 'Why Pokémon Go's technology is no fad', Brookings Institution; M. Hardy, 'Spying fears lead to Pentagon Pokémon restrictions', *Defense News* (22 July/12 August 2016); M. Pomerleau, 'Do COTS pose a threat? Rand says yes', C4ISRNet (12 July 2016); 'Snapping up cheap spy tools, nations "monitoring everyone"', Yahoo! News; J. Detsch and J. Stone, 'In aftermath of the DNC hack, experts warn of new front in digital warfare', *Christian Science Monitor* (2/10 August 2016); K. Kruithof et al., 'The role of the "dark web" in the trade of illicit drugs', Rand Corporation;

'Taking stock of the online drugs trade', Rand Corporation (2016); 'Feds: Plastic gun from 3-d printer seized at Nevada airport', *Seattle Times*; J. Boudreau and M. Ngoc Chau, 'Spyware deluge hits Vietnam sites amid South China sea spat', Bloomberg; Y. Fanusie, 'The new frontier in terror fundraising: Bitcoin', *Cipher Brief*; 'Cyber threat grows for bitcoin exchanges', Reuters (10/24/29 August 2016); D. Anderson, Q. C., *Report of the Bulk Powers Review* (August 2016).

23. Svendsen, *Understanding the Globalization of Intelligence*, p. 131; G. Corera, *Intercept* (London: Weidenfeld & Nicolson, 2015); A. Danchev, *On Good and Evil and the Grey Zone* (Edinburgh: Edinburgh University Press, 2016); J.G. Carter et al., 'Law enforcement fusion centers: Cultivating an information sharing environment while safeguarding Privacy', *Journal of Police and Criminal Psychology* (May 2016).

24. See, e.g., C. McGoogan, 'You can now find out if GCHQ spied on you', *Wired*, 'MI5 boss warns of technology terror risk', BBC; M. Hohmann, 'The German NSA affair and the need for reform in Berlin', *Lawfare* (16–17 September 2015); M. Holden, 'Online firms block terrorism investigations—Top British policeman', Reuters; E. MacAskill, 'The spooks have come out of the shadows—For now', *Guardian* (5/28 October 2015); 'IS exploits Telegram mobile app to spread propaganda', BBC; B. Quinn, 'Terror threat to UK is greater than any point in career, says MI5 chief', *Guardian*; 'MI5 boss wants 'mature debate' on surveillance powers', BBC (7/29 October 2015); 'Theresa May says 'contentious' parts of web surveillance plan dropped', BBC; 'Britain to present new watered down surveillance bill', Reuters; G. Corera, 'A new licence for spies and police?' BBC (1/3 November 2015); E. MacAskill, 'GCHQ boss calls for new relationship with tech firms over encryption', *Guardian*; B. Bergstein, 'Head of British intelligence agency on Apple, Snowden, and regrets', *MIT Technology Review* (7/11 March 2016); D. Volz, 'Reddit change sparks concerns about U.S. government spying', Reuters; P. C. Toomey, 'The Obama administration has embraced legal theories even broader than John Yoo's', *Just Security* (1/7 April 2016); B. Stevenson, 'UK committee urges more legal clarity on overseas UAV strikes', *FlightGlobal* (11 May 2016); K.B. Williams, 'Search warrant change sparks backlash', *The Hill*; D. Deptula and J. Raskas, 'Just warfare entails risk; Movie "Eye in the Sky" perverts just war laws', *Breaking Defense* (15–16 May 2016); T. Owen, 'The police can't track your cellphone without a warrant, judge rules', *VICE* (13 July 2016); D. Oberhaus, 'How the government is waging crypto war 2.0', *Motherboard*; 'France says fight against messaging encryption needs worldwide initiative', Reuters (10/11 August 2016); J. Laperruque, 'A problematic pseudo-category of surveillance information and promising post-collection policy', *Just Security* (25 August 2016).

25. On DATINT, Svendsen, *Intelligence Cooperation and the War on Terror*, p. 14; Svendsen, *Understanding the Globalization of Intelligence*, p. 84; N. Eagle and K. Greene, *Reality Mining: Data to Engineer a Better World* (Cambridge, MA: MIT Press, 2014); 'Google meets Italy's demands on data use practices', Reuters (29 July 2016); on related 'privatisation' trends, Svendsen, *The Professionalization of Intelligence Cooperation*, pp. 20–21; K.G. Coleman, 'The growing problem of data sabotage', C4IS-RNet; 'Biometric data of over 100 UK terrorism suspects lost—Watchdog', Reuters (23/27 May 2016); S. Schechner, 'Tech giants target terrorist propaganda', *Wall Street*

Journal; 'Social media giants must do more to police sites—MPs', Reuters (31 July/25 August 2016); O. Malik, 'Apple, Google, Amazon, and the advantages of bigness', *New Yorker*, 'Sage customers exposed to data breaches of their own making', Reuters; H. Rosemont, 'Public–private security cooperation: From cyber to financial crime', *RUSI* (9/18/26 August 2016).

26. On Apple/technology companies versus FBI/US government, S. Hennessey and B. Wittes, 'Apple is selling you a phone, not civil liberties', *Lawfare*; 'Bill Gates calls for terror data debate', BBC; Tucker, 'FBI head: Apple is taking us to a "different world"', *Defense One*; D. Seetharaman and J. Nicas, 'Tech companies to unite in support of Apple', *Wall Street Journal*; K.B. Williams, 'FBI director: Encryption "the hardest question I've seen in government"'; 'Lawmakers introduce compromise encryption bill', *The Hill* (18/23/25/29 February 2016); M.D. Shear, D.E. Sanger, and K. Benner, 'In the Apple case, a debate over data hits home', *New York Times*; A. Segal and A. Grigsby, 'How to break the deadlock over data encryption', *Washington Post*; B. Wittes, 'A new front in the second crypto war', *Lawfare*; K. Benner and E. Lichtblau, 'U.S. says it has unlocked iPhone without Apple'; E. Lichtblau, 'In Apple debate on digital privacy and the iPhone, questions still remain', *New York Times* (13/15/28 March 2016); S. Landau, 'Million-dollar vulnerabilities and an FBI for the twenty-first century', *Lawfare*; M. Hosenball, 'FBI paid under $1 million to unlock San Bernardino iPhone: Sources', Reuters (26/28 April 2016); N. Mott, 'Apple emphasizes users' privacy amid its parade of updates', *Christian Science Monitor*; K. Conger, 'Apple will require HTTPS connections for iOS apps by the end of 2016', *TechCrunch* (14 June 2016); A. Boyd, 'Draft encryption bill puts rule of law above privacy concerns', *Federal Times*; J. Sanchez, 'Feinstein-Burr: The bill that bans your browser', *Just Security* (8/29 April 2016); S. Sorcher, 'What the US government really thinks about encryption', *Christian Science Monitor* (25 May 2016); see also C. Davidson, 'France attacks Facebook data tracking, opening new front in privacy battles', *Christian Science Monitor* (12 February 2016); Y. Abutaleb and J. Menn, 'Egypt blocked Facebook internet service over surveillance—Sources', Reuters (1 April 2016); 'Insurers find Google a potential rival: Report', Reuters (1 March 2016).

27. See, e.g., S. Oakford, '"Snowden Treaty" aims to protect privacy, whistle-blowers—And end mass surveillance', *VICE* (24 September 2015); 'Drone leaflet drop urges agents to quit', BBC; 'Intelligence reform in a post-Snowden world', Center for Strategic and International Studies (6/9 October 2015); M. Taylor and W. Schmitt, 'Whistleblowers in defense deserve better, say lawmakers', *McClatchy* (13 June 2016); K.B. Williams, 'Intel chairs slam 'knee-jerk' opposition to cyber sharing bill', *The Hill*; K. Waddell, 'Senate passes cyber bill, ducking privacy fears for now', *Defense One* (2/28 October 2015); J. Uchill, 'Info-sharing law applies to industry as well as government, agencies say', *The Hill* (15 June 2016); A. Boyd, 'What does CTIIC actually do?' C4ISRNet (4 August 2016); C. Cordero, 'The DNI's new transparency implementation plan', *Lawfare* (27 October 2015); E. MacAskill, 'UK setting bad example on surveillance, says UN privacy chief', *Guardian* (9 March 2016). Elsewhere generating concerns, see, e.g., J.A. Cohen, 'Opinion: The insecurity underpinning Xi Jinping's repression', *Washington Post* (24 September 2015); G. Shih, 'China's crackdown raises familiar specter of foreign forces', Associated Press;

C. Gracie, 'China show trials: Victory for politics of fear in Tianjin?' BBC; U. Botobekov, 'China's nightmare: Xinjiang Jihadists go global', *Diplomat* (5/17 August 2016); P. Tucker, 'Thanks America! How China's newest software could track, predict, and crush dissent', *Defense One* (7 March 2016); I. Khrennikov, 'Putin's "Big Brother" surveillance law criticized by Snowden', Bloomberg (7 July 2016).

28. Based on paraphrased information from a non-attributable source; D. Hoffman, 'The essential link between privacy and security: Optimizing for both', *Lawfare*; C.S. Stewart and M. Maremont, 'Twitter bars intelligence agencies from using analytics service', *Wall Street Journal*; R. McCormick, 'Twitter reportedly told analytics company to stop supplying information to US intelligence agencies', *Verge* (3/8 May 2016); 'Examining ISIS support and opposition networks on Twitter', Rand Corporation; 'Twitter suspended 360,000 accounts for 'promotion of terrorism', Reuters (18 August 2016); T. Roeder, 'CIA chief talks social media for spies, government role on internet at Aspen seminar', *Colorado Springs Gazette* (31 July 2016); see also J. Cox, 'GCHQ has disclosed over 20 vulnerabilities this year, including ones in iOS', *MotherBoard* (29 April 2016); J.S. Davis, 'GCHQ infosec group disclosed kernel privilege exploit to Apple', *SC Magazine* (23 May 2016); A. Hern, 'NSA denies "Raiders of the Lost Ark" stockpile of security vulnerabilities', *Guardian*; E. Nakashima and A. Peterson, 'NSA's use of software flaws to hack foreign targets posed risks to cybersecurity', *Washington Post*; J. Vijayan, 'Zero-days: Why these security flaws are so dangerous and expensive', *Christian Science Monitor* (6/17/26 August 2016). On 'R2P' and 'public safety', see Svendsen, *Intelligence Cooperation and the War on Terror*, p. 40, p. 63, p. 72, p. 93, p. 100, p. 173; Svendsen, *Understanding the Globalization of Intelligence*, p. 237, col. 2; Svendsen, *The Professionalization of Intelligence Cooperation*, p. 243, col. 1; J. Binnie, 'UNMISS under investigation for failing to protect civilians', IHS Jane's 360 (17 August 2016).

29. See, e.g., D. Howarth, *Law as Engineering* (Cheltenham: Edward Elgar, 2013)—I am indebted to Dr Nóra Ní Loideain of the University of Cambridge for drawing this source to my attention; see also N. Ni Loideain, 'National mass communications data surveillance and the law', *CRASSH* (9 August 2016); Anderson, *A Question of Trust* (2015); Svendsen, '"Smart Law" for intelligence!'; Anderson, *Report of the Bulk Powers Review* (2016).

30. See also as outlined in Svendsen, 'Intelligence, surveillance and reconnaissance (ISR)'.

31. See chapter 5; see also warnings in L.M. Krauss, 'Trump's anti-science campaign', *New Yorker* (21 August 2016).

32. On 'blowback', Svendsen, *Intelligence Cooperation and the War on Terror*, p. 22, p. 104, p. 110, p. 147, p. 162, p. 169; Svendsen, *Understanding the Globalization of Intelligence*, p. 10, p. 22, p. 33, p. 62, p. 88, p. 110, p. 124, p. 147, p. 152; Svendsen, *The Professionalization of Intelligence Cooperation*, p. 25, p. 137, p. 146.

Chapter Two

Intelligence as 'Art' and 'Science'

FROM FOUNDATIONS TO FRAMEWORKS

The purpose of this chapter is to, firstly, provide a brief survey of the key recent literature focused on the nature of intelligence, particularly as it reflects
the 'art' and 'science' disciplines. Next, building on that discussion, general
insights into further extending engineering realms and how engineering more
specifically relates to intelligence are then offered. Drawing on the definitions provided in chapter 1, and going to the core of what engineering means
with regard to intelligence, these insights aim to better probe the intelligence-
engineering nexus and relationships, while providing further insight into the
nature and characteristics of IE.

LAUNCHPAD-RELATED KICK-OFFS

There is little dispute that intelligence, and particularly its more specific
dimensions—such as notably intelligence analysis—has been long and substantially conceptualised as reflecting both the 'art' and 'science' disciplines
in its composition and behaviour. Thus, while extents may vary, intelligence
is considerably recognised as 'an art' and 'a science' in how it is done and in
how intelligence practitioners go about their business. Frequently and most
ideally, a balance emerges between the domains of the arts and sciences,
and—at least arguably, as the definitions of engineering presented in chapter
1 indicate—this is where IE can build most satisfactorily.[1] As has been noted
elsewhere, 'a skilful combination of these two processes [the 'artistic' and
the 'scientific'] is the essence of modern intelligence analysis'.[2] We begin by
reviewing intelligence as an art.

INTELLIGENCE AS AN 'ART'

To regard intelligence as an 'art', first it is most helpful if we briefly evaluate the term 'art', which is itself not an uncontested entity. Resonating most closely with work conducted in human intelligence (HUMINT) domains of intelligence activity, and with regard to humans and the behaviour they exhibit, the *OED* defines 'art' as

> noun
> 1 [mass noun] the expression or application of human creative skill and imagination, typically in a visual form . . .
> • works produced by human creative skill and imagination . . .
>   creative activity resulting in the production of [something (in this case usage, read, for example, intelligence reports as being representative of intelligence products)] . . .
> • a skill at doing a specified thing, typically one acquired through practice.[3]

When discussing 'artistic attributes' with regard to more specific intelligence analysis efforts, UK intelligence educator Julian Richards highlights 'the cognitive activities surrounding analysis itself, with a view to raising awareness about these activities (which can be called *heuristics*), and considering how to mitigate their negative aspects'. He continues, 'This, in a sense, is the "art" part of the picture'.[4]

Later, in a chapter titled 'Analytical Theory: The Art of Analysis', Richards goes on to examine intellectual and philosophical themes, including critical thinking, creativity, judgement, and communication, demonstrating what he includes in his purview of intelligence as art. The human mind and its cognitive activities, both conscious and unconscious, figure centrally.[5] As he concludes, 'On the art side of the picture is the question of the nature of analysis itself, and particularly issues of how human beings charged with undertaking intelligence analysis are able to deal with large amounts of complex data and derive judgements'.[6]

PAINTING RATHER THAN PHOTOGRAPHY

Associated evaluations have gone further. In a 2012 article, former CIA intelligence analyst Stephen Marrin drew on similar key themes, again in the more specific intelligence analysis context. He asked, 'Is intelligence analysis an art or a science?' and he underscored that 'a discussion, sometimes portrayed as a debate, has been taking place for decades addressing the issue of whether intelligence analysis is an art or a science.'[7] He draws on the work of Robert

Folker, where Folker asks 'whether intelligence analysis should be accepted as an art (depending largely on subjective intuitive judgment) or a science (depending largely on structured, systemic analytic methods)'.[8]

Why the above queries are important and why we should care, better answering the *So what?* question, is equally revealed by Marrin: 'The answer to this question [Is intelligence analysis an art or a science?] has significant implications for the selection, training, and career development of intelligence analysts, as well as the actual methodologies of intelligence analysis'.[9] These concerns, therefore, are not so abstract that they can be dismissed, and evidently they cannot afford to be overlooked in practical terms. This is not only with regard to intelligence and its analysis but also with relevance to the full spectrum of intelligence activities that exist more widely, such as with substantially fused intelligence collection/gathering efforts. Ultimately, we see that both qualitative and quantitative factors and considerations figure centrally both in and with regard to intelligence enterprises as they are understood most fully.[10]

Increasingly linked to the 'science' side of the overall intelligence equation or spectrum, as Richards notes, 'an examination of the analysis process itself quickly leads into a number of other academic disciplines, from cognitive psychology to social and behavioural science'. He also notably remarks that 'advanced skills in communication . . . must also be seen as a critical component of the analyst's "soft skills" in delivering their capability'.[11] These communication skills for conveying at a minimum data-to-information, information-to-intelligence, intelligence-to-knowledge, and knowledge-to-wisdom—which, in turn, have been processed through a series of 'intelligence cycles'—are vital to the important intelligence producer-end user relationship. Various forms of 'narrative' and 'discourse' similarly boast significance within this area.[12]

INTELLIGENCE AS A 'SCIENCE'

A baseline definition of 'science' similarly stands out as helpful for seeing where intelligence 'fits' into the overall schema. The *OED* defines 'science' as

noun [mass noun]
the intellectual and practical activity encompassing the systematic study of the structure and behaviour of the physical and natural world through observation and experiment . . .
• a systematically organized body of knowledge on a particular subject.[13]

For Richards, 'the "science" part of intelligence analysis, namely the technical and organisational considerations which surround the analysis process

. . . can help, if used correctly'—one could also read here, if used *system-atically* and *methodologically*—'to enhance the overall effectiveness of the process and mitigate against failures'.[14] Meanwhile, U.S. physicist James O. Weatherall argues appropriately that science is 'a way of learning about the world—an ongoing process of discovery, testing, and revision'.[15] Thinking in terms of experiments and their attendant variables, whether independent or not, brings this out more clearly. Greater *structuring* and refined *focus* in these activities becomes notably more prominent when more 'scientific' approaches to intelligence are adopted.[16]

Richards concludes,

> Scientific approaches to intelligence analysis primarily comprise systematic methods for organising and sorting data, and for generating and testing hypotheses, which have the dual purpose of overcoming the natural frailties and biases of the human brain, and of allowing critical and creative thinking to take place. Such methods range from generating and challenging alternative hypotheses and models, to analysing complex networks of individuals and their degree of interrelationship using techniques derived from scientific and mathematical approaches to mining and analysing very large datasets. In this sense, intelligence can be seen as something of a branch of scientific enquiry, floating somewhere between natural and social science, and mathematics and statistical analysis.[17]

This highly diverse and empowering 'scientific' nature of intelligence is effectively reflected in the sheer array of different approaches and methodologies present throughout intelligence work. As already seen, this is especially apparent amid those approaches and methods that are generally found, for example, in the literature focused on the more specific intelligence activities of *intelligence analysis*. This is particularly evident in how-to and handbook-type guides, which are useful for teaching students of intelligence and for training intelligence analysts. Both intelligence newcomers and more experienced professionals soon gain.[18]

PHOTOGRAPHY RATHER THAN PAINTING

As the literature on intelligence has rapidly developed over the last few decades in both volume and detail (including, at least at times, in terms of quality), many authors have increasingly poured over the theme of intelligence '*as* a science' as well as its relationship *between* and *to* science and the sciences as subjects. These authors have also extracted and presented at length many valuable policy-relevant insights.[19] When exploring science in relation to intelligence, the dimensions of both 'hard' (physical) and 'soft' (social) sciences emerge with greater clarity. This is especially apparent in the *OED*'s definition of 'social science' captured as 'the scientific study of human society and social relationships'.[20] Human factors remain central.

More broadly, events and developments in relation to intelligence have similarly been 'rationalized as the "scientization of intelligence"',[21] hinting at processes undergone both for and with regard to intelligence. Hand-in-glove over time, intelligence (as an entity) has become increasingly 'scientifically managed', which has been seen most instructively throughout history in the case of industrialised-to-automated handling of technical intelligence (TECHINT) and its derivative signals intelligence (SIGINT) during World War II and in the years since.[22]

However, there has been some dispute over the—at least perceived—'scientific' dimensions of intelligence, as argued by the *Economist* in March 2005: 'The comforting idea that technology would make spying more of a high-tech science was blown apart by September 11th and the Iraq fiasco [the Iraq War, 2003]'. The *Economist* continued with the assertion that spying more broadly 'is now a more risky, more human affair where real eyes and ears matter'.[23] A degree of re-balancing was necessary.

A QUESTION OF BALANCE

The insights presented above emphasise that 'human' and 'artistic factors' can by no means be taken out of the overall equation of intelligence work. This contention somewhat overlaps with long-standing, varying, and overarching technical intelligence (TECHINT) vis-à-vis—even versus—human intelligence (HUMINT) debates, while extending to tactical/operations intelligence (TACINT/OPINT) vis-à-vis and versus strategic intelligence (STRATINT), military intelligence (MILINT/MI), and defence intelligence (DEFINT/DI) balance or imbalance arguments that continue to exist in the intelligence world. This is most notable when we examine the domain of intelligence more generally and comprehensively over different timescales and locations.[24]

Ultimately, intelligence and its products—consisting of, most ideally, an optimum mix of '*empirical and interpretive extrapolations*'—come to the fore.[25] Thus we find that as we extend intelligence processes to strategic futures work,

> the artistic and scientific dimensions of intelligence should be given equal weighting. This is so that synergy, arising from the fusion of both dimensions, can be

maximized. Moreover, this is undertaken so that those issues not so highlighted are not neglected or overlooked. In summary, the overall process should work by prioritizing like a medical 'triage' system.[26]

Thereby, we can also further refine essential intelligence activities, such as targeting and prioritisation.[27] Effectively building on this foundation of a fusion between art *and* science, the relationship between intelligence and engineering is now examined in greater depth.

THE INTELLIGENCE-ENGINEERING NEXUS

As contended elsewhere, contemporary intelligence is moving beyond the general disciplines of the 'arts' and the 'sciences' and into more specific 'engineering' realms. Particularly key for discernible intelligence engineering and architectural design processes, as Professor David Blockley has argued, is the fact that 'in the twenty-first century, we are beginning to understand how complex behaviour can emerge from interactions between many simpler highly interconnected processes'. Blockley goes on to argue, 'Every hard [physical] system is embedded in a soft system—ultimately all of us. . . . Systems thinking is helping us to integrate disparate specialisms by seeing tools as physical "manipulators" of energy embedded in "soft" people systems'. Intelligence processes and associated enterprises, as they encounter similar challenges, can learn several communicable lessons. Those lessons are applicable both in and across technical intelligence (TECHINT) and human intelligence (HUMINT) domains.

Blockley continues, 'If we are to make and maintain highly reliable and sustainable complex systems, then we need more of our specialist engineers to be systems thinkers that can deal with the detail and the big picture—a synergy from the integration of reductionism and holism'. The same argument considerably resonates for contemporary intelligence practitioners, or indeed anyone involved with managing critical information flows, as they seek to navigate the highly complex environments, introduced above, as successfully as possible and with most balance.[28]

Although exact balances in precise circumstances and at particular points in time and space might be challenged, the multidisciplinary essence of intelligence is little contested. There is a strong natural relationship between intelligence and engineering. This relationship, involving nurturing characteristics, both builds on and overlaps with how the intelligence-related 'art' and 'science' dimensions both conventionally and generally relate to engineering.[29]

ENGINEERING *AND* INTELLIGENCE

Engineering Policy Advisor Natasha McCarthy, in a characterisation of the nature of engineering, offers further areas where the relationship of intelligence to engineering can be better elicited and then further elucidated. When intelligence activities are taken at their widest, as in chapter 1, McCarthy illustrates appropriate areas of harmony in her claim that 'engineering encompasses an extremely broad range of activities on a whole spectrum of levels'.[30] Moreover, particularly with an eye to a range of infrastructures and their management, there is a demonstrable and prevailing 'sense of the role of engineering in shaping lifestyle, culture, society, knowledge—as great a role perhaps as the more often lauded sciences and arts'.[31]

We should not overlook or neglect engineering aspects with regard to intelligence and its associated activities. This is especially relevant because over time, 'engineering specialisms were created by existing crafts and trades developing into engineering disciplines through the introduction of engineering method'.[32] Alternative problem-solving, or trouble-shooting, approaches equally matter and contribute in harmony with the engineering methodologies increasingly adopted by intelligence through their greater functional harnessing.[33]

Once more highlighting the strong linkage of engineering to 'art' and 'science', with similar implications for more specific intelligence interests, McCarthy notes that 'the actual design process in engineering . . . [involves] both appreciation of . . . scientific theory and its limits and an understanding of what applications are needed and are likely to be successful'. This further highlights the applicability of intelligence-relevant aspects such as vision and creativity, for instance, during the real-time or live conduct of operations.[34] Similarly, as McCarthy cautions, 'it is important not to put too much weight on distinctions between science and engineering. . . . The two are not the different sides of a coin but the ends of a spectrum, and much lies between the two extremes'.[35] Any artifices, therefore, should not distort and should be mitigated as far as is possible. Much is grey, and perhaps a fortiori, in the famously 'smoke and mirrors' world of intelligence where degrees of deception, even betrayal, often lurk in the shadows.[36]

There is substantial intrigue as regards intelligence and IE. Delving deeper, and demonstrating that an evolving area of more specific IE is not a surprising development—and is, in fact, no exception in contemporary circumstances, thereby further highlighting its current timeliness and claimed relevance—McCarthy remarks, 'The engineering profession is like a life form that keeps evolving into distinct species as new niches appear. Developments in technology and even changes in society often lead to the creation of a new, distinct branch of engineering'.[37] Furthermore, emphasising continual conditions of change over stasis, change that can occur at ever-faster rates of necessarily well-informed turnover and turnaround, she notes, 'The fact that engineering is so focused on human needs means that engineers need to have an understanding of the nature of human needs and desires, and how to create artifacts that successfully meet those needs and which are easily used. This is quite some challenge'.[38] Intelligence and its activities figure centrally here, recalling William J. ('Wild Bill') Donovan's still-relevant comment in a 1941 memorandum to President Franklin D. Roosevelt: 'Strategy, without information upon which it can rely, is helpless'.[39]

FROM KNOWLEDGE TO ACTION, AND BACK

More pointedly, building on those earlier conditions of knowledge informing work and vice versa, McCarthy notes, 'Engineers should never be satisfied with the way things are'.[40] This echoes previous research that has found that 'perhaps more constructively and boasting something intelligence operatives have to, and should ideally, share, system engineers "must have *skeptical positive thinking* as a prerequisite to *prudent risk taking*"'.[41]

Indeed, effectively demonstrating the range of complexities encountered, McCarthy maintains her characterisation of the engineering world when she says, 'Engineers are increasingly involved in the building of *systems*. . . . Engineers are involved in the design of complex systems with many parts, each of which has to be developed by specialists, but with an eye on how they fit into the whole',[42] while underscoring the fact that 'the ability to think in terms of and to design systems with interrelated and technologically diverse parts is *integral to modern defence*'.[43] The relationship to sophisticated federation/system of systems thinking and closely associated tasks, such as particularly those undertaken by special operational forces (SOF), becomes increasingly obvious. Equally, more 'multiplexic' terms resonate, drawing on common definitions.[44]

Continuing more broadly in relation to defence and global security, McCarthy reveals, 'Engineers have developed an increasingly sophisticated understanding of complex systems, and the techniques developed for describing and modelling such systems can potentially play a huge role'.[45] Nowhere is this perhaps more apparent today than in the more virtually ranging domain of cyberspace. This is particularly when 'cyber' is (1) taken as a domain in itself, and when cyber is (2) linking or securing all of the other (physical) domains that exist, such as sea, air, land and space, while including attendant nuclear risk considerations.[46] Weapons of mass destruction (associated chemical, biological, radiological, nuclear and [high-yield] explosives; CBRNE), conventional arms/weapons/explosives, associated delivery systems (e.g., missiles), and/or their neutralisation/disabling concerns all continue to remain high on various intelligence and defence/security agendas.[47]

Maintaining a descriptive list of engineering features that deservedly figure with regard to intelligence work, McCarthy remarks, 'Key to engineering is the ability to assess and to manage the risks inherent in any engineered artifact, process or system'.[48] Likewise, overlapping with similar conditions and statuses in the intelligence domain, such as instances of *intelligence expectations* (how 'realistic' they are) and *intelligence failures* (that they are 'inevitable' somewhere and at some time or another), 'engineered systems should be designed to withstand uncertain future situations. . . . This is the ideal, of course, and not all engineered systems will be perfect. Failure is a fact of life'. McCarthy also re-emphasises that 'engineers often become frustrated because their understanding of risk does not tally with the public's perception'.[49] This emerges as another attribute that intelligence and its experienced practitioners commonly share, especially as they frequently operate beyond the boundaries of the conventional.[50]

FURTHER IMPACTING RAMIFICATIONS

McCarthy also introduces the legal and law-related dimensions that require greater consideration. In her treatise on engineering, McCarthy reiterates that 'engineers are becoming ever more keenly aware of the wider implications of their work and great effort has been invested over decades producing codes of ethics'.[51] This doctrine-imbued codification work has been undertaken for conduct and 'best practices' purposes, amongst other areas of utility, for instance relating to standards and the harnessing of standardisation processes in operations and other IE-related work beyond.[52] McCarthy shows the mirrored depths and breadth of this work as regards intelligence: 'Because engineers work on complex problems in a complex world, they need to make use of knowledge about nature, about society and its conventions and even the way individuals' minds work'.[53] Closely associated 'intelligence and security reach' concepts that relate to conditions of *overreach* and/or *underreach* similarly stand out for consideration, while 'proportionality' and 'necessity' concerns again figure prominently.[54]

Underlining relevant 'scholar-practitioner' characteristics—notably while applying knowledge and practical prowess in practice and/or in action—and once more articulating something that arguably should at least be equally boasted by intelligence officers, McCarthy claims, 'It is *know-how* . . . that makes engineering knowledge unique'. Indeed, 'engineers differ from scientists in that they *not only have an understanding of mathematics and physical theory*, but they also *know how to apply that understanding*'.[55] These activities span the theory-to-practice continuum with much equal note for intelligence and further extending IE enterprises.

Ultimately, as this brief survey relating to engineering demonstrates, several diverse areas of human and technical/technological activity are spanned. This coverage likewise echoes both strongly and loudly with regard to more intelligence-specific HUMINT and TECHINT extending to TACINT, OPINT, STRATINT, and MILINT/MI to DEFINT/DI endeavours. As IE is further advanced, overall efforts move from (1) roughly sketched out ideas and plans to (2) being more realistically launched and tangibly progressed in terms of the subsequent implementation and operationalisation of those ideas and plans.

CONCLUSIONS

Drawing on key recent intelligence studies which both highlight and distil the 'artistic' and 'scientific' dimensions of intelligence while referring to a comprehensive overview of engineering, this chapter provides several further insights into the more specific phenomenon of IE. The background covered also demonstrates what can be regarded as the core nature and characteristics of IE, including the several realms that concern it.

IE is not divorced from—and indeed, as can be empirically observed, it both directly and more indirectly or circuitously emerges from—its roots in the arts and sciences. In turn, these dimensions are convincingly not mutually exclusive. Neither should these aspects be so, for otherwise many damaging disconnects have great potential for emerging with serious ramifications—for example, in the counter-terrorism, counter-proliferation, counter-radicalisation, and counter–violent extremism (CVE) realms that significantly preoccupy contemporary intelligence and security communities across the world.[56]

Next, follows a discussion of IE in practice, or action, and how it can—and, more arguably, even should—be 'done' or accomplished both today and in the future.

NOTES

1. For background, see, e.g., A.D.M. Svendsen, *Understanding the Globalization of Intelligence* (Basingstoke, UK: Palgrave Macmillan, 2012), p. 63; A.D.M. Svendsen, *The Professionalization of Intelligence Cooperation* (Basingstoke, UK: Palgrave

Macmillan, 2012), pp. 155–56; E. Kleinsmith, 'Is intelligence an art or a science?' *In Public Safety* (13 May 2016).

2. J. Richards, *The Art and Science of Intelligence Analysis* (Oxford: Oxford University Press, 2010), p. 187; J-M. Palacios, 'Intelligence analysis training: A European perspective', *International Journal of Intelligence, Security, and Public Affairs*, 18, 1 (2016), pp. 34–56.

3. 'Art' definition from the *Oxford Dictionary of English* (2015); B. Stewart and S. Newbery, *Why Spy?* (London: Hurst, 2015); F.M.J. Lichacz and R. Jassemi-Zargani, *Human Factors and Intelligence, Surveillance, and Reconnaissance* (Ottawa, Canada: DR&DC, April 2016).

4. Richards, *The Art and Science of Intelligence Analysis*, p. 97; see also, notably, R. Heuer, *Psychology of Intelligence Analysis* (Washington, DC: CIA CSI, 1999); Svendsen, *The Professionalization of Intelligence Cooperation*, p. 57; A.D.M. Svendsen, 'Painting rather than photography', *Journal of Transatlantic Studies*, 7, 1 (2009), p. 15.

5. Richards, *The Art and Science of Intelligence Analysis*, pp. 98–117.

6. *Ibid.*, p. 117.

7. S. Marrin, 'Is intelligence analysis an art or a science?' *International Journal of Intelligence and CounterIntelligence*, 25, 3 (2012), p. 529.

8. Folker quoted in Marrin, 'Is intelligence analysis an art or a science?' p. 529.

9. Marrin, 'Is intelligence analysis an art or a science?' p. 529.

10. See, e.g., M.M. Lowenthal and R.M. Clark, *The Five Disciplines of Intelligence Collection* (Washington, DC: CQ Press, 2015); M.M. Lowenthal, *Intelligence* (Washington, DC: CQ Press, 2015 [6th ed.]); R.M. Clark, *Intelligence Analysis* (Washington, DC: CQ Press, 2012 [4th ed.]); W.M. Hall and G. Citrenbaum, *Intelligence Analysis* (Santa Barbara, CA: Praeger Security International, 2010); R.M. Clark, *Intelligence Collection* (Washington, DC: CQ Press, 2013); W.M. Hall and G. Citrenbaum, *Intelligence Collection* (Santa Barbara, CA: Praeger Security International, 2012).

11. Richards, *The Art and Science of Intelligence Analysis*, pp. 118–19; D. Paletta, 'Social media posts now fair game in security clearance process', *Wall Street Journal* (13 May 2016).

12. On these features, Svendsen, *Understanding the Globalization of Intelligence*, esp. p. 15, p. 89, p. 101, p. 129; Svendsen, *The Professionalization of Intelligence Cooperation*, p. 113; R. Arcos and R. Pherson, eds., *Intelligence Communication in the Digital Era* (Basingstoke, UK: Palgrave Macmillan, 2015); B. Holmes and M. Greenlee, 'More art than science: Intelligence and technical topics', *War on the Rocks* (12 April 2016); R. Perez, 'Turning data into actionable intelligence', *SC Magazine* (27 May 2016); M. Clunies Ross, 'Guide to the classics: The Icelandic saga', *The Conversation* (14 August 2016); 'M. Ravindranath, 'Ransomware 101: FBI's education effort', Nextgov.com; 'Australia unveils "how-to" guide to fight militant propaganda', Reuters (26/29 August 2016).

13. 'Science' definition from the *Oxford Dictionary of English* (2015).

14. Richards, *The Art and Science of Intelligence Analysis*, p. 97.

15. J.O. Weatherall, *The Physics of Finance—Predicting the Unpredictable* (London: Short Books, 2014), p. 205; A. Swanson, 'Wonkblog: The eerie math that could predict terrorist attacks', *Washington Post* (1 March 2016).

16. See also A.D.M. Svendsen, '"Smart law" for intelligence!', *Tech & Law Center* (University of Milan, Italy: June 2015); S. Reeves and W. Williams, 'Time for a national security expert on the Supreme Court', *Lawfare* (1 March 2016).

17. Richards, *The Art and Science of Intelligence Analysis*, p. 142, see also pp.121-142; A. Barnes, 'Making intelligence analysis more intelligent: Using numeric probabilities', *Intelligence and National Security* (2015); J. Richards, 'Competing hypotheses in contemporary intelligence analysis', chapter 2; D. Omand, 'Understanding Bayesian thinking: Prior and posterior probabilities and analysis of competing hypotheses in intelligence analysis', chapter 12 in W.J. Lahneman and R. Arcos, eds., *The Art of Intelligence* (New York: Rowman & Littlefield, 2014); 'Hypothesis generation and testing', chapter 7 of R.J. Heuer, Jr. and R.H. Pherson, *Structured Analytic Techniques for Intelligence Analysis* (Washington, DC: CQ Press, 2014 [2 ed.]).

18. See, e.g., Heuer, Jr. and Pherson, *Structured Analytic Techniques for Intelligence Analysis*; S.M. Beebe and R.H. Pherson, *Cases in Intelligence Analysis* (Washington, DC: CQ Press, 2012); R.M. Clark and W.L. Mitchell, *Target-Centric Network Modeling* (Washington, DC: CQ Press, 2015); R. Dover and M.S. Goodman, eds., *Learning from the Secret Past* (Washington, DC: Georgetown University Press, 2011); see also wider methodology and approach-related discussions in Svendsen, *The Professionalization of Intelligence Cooperation*, from p. 43.

19. W. Agrell and G.F. Treverton, *National Intelligence and Science* (Oxford: Oxford University Press, 2015); W. Agrell and G.F. Treverton, 'The science of intelligence: Reflections on a field that never was', chapter 11 in W. Agrell and G.F. Treverton, eds., *National Intelligence Systems* (Cambridge: Cambridge University Press, 2009); Svendsen, *The Professionalization of Intelligence Cooperation*, p. 155.

20. 'Social Science' definition from the *Oxford Dictionary of English* (2015); for how these 'soft' and 'hard' science debates intersect with theory and theoretical considerations in the domain of intelligence evaluation, see Svendsen, *The Professionalization of Intelligence Cooperation*, pp. 58–59.

21. Svendsen, *Understanding the Globalization of Intelligence*, p. 129.

22. Svendsen, *The Professionalization of Intelligence Cooperation*, p. 18; A.D.M. Svendsen, 'Buffeted not busted: The UKUSA "five eyes" after Snowden', *e-IR.info* (8 January 2014); G. Corera, 'How the British and Americans started listening in', BBC (8 February 2016); G. Corera, *Intercept* (London: Weidenfeld & Nicolson, 2015); A.M. Rutkowski, 'International signals intelligence law: Provisions and history', *Lawfare*, 4, 1 (March 2016); R.V. Jones, *Most Secret War* (London: Hamish Hamilton, 1978).

23. As quoted in A.D.M. Svendsen, *Intelligence Cooperation and the War on Terror* (London: Routledge, 2010), pp. 49–50; S. Hughes, 'To stop ISIS recruitment, focus offline', *Lawfare* (7 August 2016).

24. See these debates in A.D.M. Svendsen, 'Intelligence, surveillance and reconnaissance (ISR)', in J. Deni and D. Galbreath, eds., *The Routledge Handbook of Defence Studies* (London: Routledge, forthcoming); Svendsen, *Intelligence Cooperation and the War on Terror*, p. 27; for OPINT vs. STRATINT balancing concerns, see A.D.M. Svendsen, 'Developing international intelligence liaison against Islamic State', *International Journal of Intelligence and CounterIntelligence*, 29, 2 (2016),

pp. 260–77; K. Wong, 'US commander: Lack of intelligence assets slowing down ISIS war', *The Hill* (7 June 2016); P.H.J. Davies, 'The problem of defence intelligence', *Intelligence and National Security* (2016); J. Thomson, 'Governance costs and defence intelligence provision in the UK: A case-study in microeconomic theory', *Intelligence and National Security* (2015); P.B. Symon and A. Tarapore, 'Defense intelligence analysis in the age of big data', *Joint Forces Quarterly*, 79 (2015), pp. 4–11; P. Osborne, 'Defence intelligence: Increasingly different today and tomorrow', *RUSI Video*; M. Pomerleau, 'Technology's impact on intelligence collection', *The Hill* (1/18 March 2016); A.D.M. Svendsen, 'Contemporary intelligence innovation in practice', *Defence Studies*, 15, 2 (2015), p. 107; N. Duckworth, 'Cyber's hot, but low-tech spies are still a threat', *National Interest*; J. Zager and R. Zager, 'Improving cybersecurity through human systems integration', *Small Wars Journal* (22 August 2016); B.A. Lewis, 'The death of human Intelligence', *Military and Strategic Affairs*, 8, 1 (July 2016), pp. 75–90; D. Harris, 'The consequences of eroding human intelligence collection', *Cipher Brief* (2 November 2016).

25. Svendsen, *Understanding the Globalization of Intelligence*, p. 116; Svendsen, *The Professionalization of Intelligence Cooperation*, p. 59.

26. Svendsen, *Understanding the Globalization of Intelligence*, p. 132; K. DeYoung, 'U.S. intelligence officials: Venezuela could be headed for collapse', *Washington Post* (13 May 2016).

27. On targeting, e.g., A.D.M. Svendsen, 'Advancing "defence-in-depth": Intelligence and systems dynamics', *Defense & Security Analysis*, 31, 1 (2015), p. 67; Svendsen, *Intelligence Cooperation and the War on Terror*, esp., p. 59, p. 93, p. 98; Svendsen, *Understanding the Globalization of Intelligence*, esp., p. 6, p. 71, p. 78, p. 89, p. 94, p. 101, p. 115, p. 129, pp. 131–32; Svendsen, *The Professionalization of Intelligence Cooperation*, esp. p. 121, p. 126, p. 147, p. 152, p. 157; '4.7 Ranking, scoring, prioritizing' in 'decomposition and visualization' chapter 4 in Heuer, Jr. and Pherson, *Structured Analytic Techniques for Intelligence Analysis*.

28. Svendsen, 'Advancing "defence-in-depth"', p. 59; also for more intelligence-relevant insights relating to 'engineering', D. Blockley, *Engineering* (Oxford: Oxford University Press, 2012); C. Clark, 'NGA, NRO, NSA joining DoD in Silicon Valley', *Breaking Defense* (16 May 2016); E. Lake, 'Orders for U.S. forces in Syria: "Don't get shot"', Bloomberg (11 August 2016).

29. For the 'multi-everything' nature of intelligence, see the Introduction to this book.

30. N. McCarthy, *Engineering* (London: Oneworld, 2009), p. vi; for multilevels of experience and analysis in intelligence domains, see as elaborated further in chapter 3; see also Svendsen, *Understanding the Globalization of Intelligence*, p. 12; insights in Svendsen, *Intelligence Cooperation and the War on Terror*, pp. 167–73.

31. McCarthy, *Engineering*, p. viii; on 'shaping' in intelligence contexts, e.g., Svendsen, *The Professionalization of Intelligence Cooperation*, p. 121, p. 162; on 'infrastructures', Svendsen, 'Advancing "defence-in-depth"', pp. 63–64.

32. McCarthy, *Engineering*, p. 24; on intelligence 'tradecraft', Svendsen, *Understanding the Globalization of Intelligence*, p. 119; Svendsen, *The Professionalization of Intelligence Cooperation*, p. 22, p. 50, pp. 143–44, p. 148; Svendsen, *Intelligence Cooperation and the War on Terror*, p. 127, p. 143.

33. For the importance of adopting different approaches to intelligence-relevant acute 'problem-solving' or 'trouble-shooting', e.g., Svendsen, *The Professionalization of Intelligence Cooperation*, esp. p. 123, p. 132, p. 158; Svendsen, *Understanding the Globalization of Intelligence*, esp. p. 6, p. 29, p. 73, p. 78; J. Judson, 'USSOCOM: "Transregional" approach needed to combat ISIS', *Defense News* (9 May 2016).

34. McCarthy, *Engineering*, p. 16; for declassified, historic examples of 'creativity' being encouraged at the CIA, e.g., Svendsen, *The Professionalization of Intelligence Cooperation*, p. 89, p. 91, p. 93; Svendsen, *Intelligence Cooperation and the War on Terror*, p. 169.

35. McCarthy, *Engineering*, p. 19.

36. Svendsen, *The Professionalization of Intelligence Cooperation*, p. 135; classic texts are E. Montagu, *The Man Who Never Was* (London: Penguin, 1956 [1953]); and J.C. Masterman, *The Double Cross System* (London: Sphere, 1973 [1972]); for more recent examples, R. Finegan, 'Shadowboxing in the dark', *Terrorism and Political Violence*, 28, 3 (2016), pp. 497–519; S. Swann and D. Casciani, 'Going undercover against extremism', BBC (18 August 2016); A. French, 'The plot to take down a Fox News analyst', *New York Times*; 'Former Fox News commentator sentenced to prison for faking CIA ties', Reuters (15 July 2016); Svendsen, *Understanding the Globalization of Intelligence*, p. 7; A.K. Sen, 'Distract, deceive, destroy: Atlantic Council report exposes Putin's deceptions in Syria', Atlantic Council (5 April 2016); M. Czuperski et al., *Distract Deceive Destroy* (Washington, DC: Atlantic Council, 2016); K. Pynnöniemi and A. Rácz (eds.), *Fog of Falsehood* (Helsinki: FIIA, May 2016); C. Paul and M. Matthews, 'The Russian "firehose of falsehood" propaganda model', Rand Corporation (2016); R. Dannenberg, 'Russia: Deception and deniability', *Cipher Brief* (21 July 2016); A. Ostrovsky, 'Opinion: For Putin, disinformation is power', *New York Times*, B. Whitmore, 'Podcast: Spies, lies, head games', Radio Free Europe/Radio Liberty; C. Bennett, 'Democrats' new warning: Leaks could include Russian lies', *Politico* (5/17 August 2016); as noted in the introduction, much contemporary skepticism remains relating to, e.g., Snowden and to many associated unanswered questions; A. Gibney, 'Can we trust Julian Assange and WikiLeaks?'; 'Is WikiLeaks putting people at risk?' BBC; A.E. Kramer, 'More of Kremlin's opponents are ending up dead', *New York Times*; 'Assange says WikiLeaks to release "significant" Clinton campaign data', Reuters (8/23/20/25 August 2016).

37. McCarthy, *Engineering*, p. 13; A.E. Berman and J. Dornier, 'Technology feels like it's accelerating—Because it actually is', *Singularity Hub* (22 March 2016).

38. McCarthy, *Engineering*, pp. 14–15.

39. Quoted in Svendsen, *The Professionalization of Intelligence Cooperation*, p. 3; R.Z. George, 'Intelligence and Strategy', chapter 8 in J. Baylis et al., eds., *Strategy in the Contemporary World* (Oxford: Oxford University Press, 2016 [5th ed.]), esp. p. 137; K. Ayoub and K. Payne, 'Strategy in the age of artificial intelligence', *Journal of Strategic Studies* (November 2015).

40. McCarthy, *Engineering*, p. 15; see also under subheading, 'From "building-blocks" to "game-changers"' in Svendsen, 'Advancing "defence-in-depth"', from p. 64.

41. *Ibid.*, p. 61 (emphasis added); A. Baunov, 'A well-timed retreat: Russia pulls back from Syria', Carnegie Moscow; 'Putin's surprise withdrawal', Soufan Group

(15–16 March 2016); M. Mazzetti, A. Barnard, and E. Schmitt, 'Military success in Syria gives Putin upper hand in U.S. proxy war', *New York Times*, 'A strong statement by Russia', Soufan Group; J.D. Durso, 'Russia is winning the war before the war', *Real Clear Defense*; A.E. Kramer and A. Barnard, 'Russia asserts its military might in Syria', *New York Times* (6/17/19 August 2016); G. Dominguez, 'Chinese military to step up "training, humanitarian aid" to Syria'; F. Abi Ali, 'Russia projects power into gulf and east Mediterranean at expense of US and allies', IHS Jane's 360 (19/22 August 2016); B. Renz, 'Why Russia is reviving its conventional military power', *Parameters*, 46, 2 (2016), pp. 23–36. More conversely, D. Gambetta and S. Hertog, 'Uncivil engineers', *Foreign Affairs* (10 March 2016); Svendsen, *Intelligence Cooperation and the War on Terror*, esp. pp. 97–99.

42. McCarthy, *Engineering*, p. 74 (emphasis in original); see discussion of intelligence systems and their attributes/variables in esp. Svendsen, *Understanding the Globalization of Intelligence*, pp. 99–107; Svendsen, *The Professionalization of Intelligence Cooperation*, p. 19, p. 25, p. 60, p. 140, pp. 141–42; for intelligence systems in action/practice, see Svendsen, *Intelligence Cooperation and the War on Terror*, esp. p. 28; for further insights into the rich systems and systems engineering literatures that exist and extending to covering complex 'federation/system of systems' implications with regard and relevance to intelligence, see throughout, inter alia, Svendsen, 'Advancing "defence-in-depth"', pp. 58–73; Svendsen, 'Contemporary intelligence innovation in practice', pp. 105–23; A.D.M. Svendsen, 'Making it STARC! Proposed future ways forward for contemporary military and special operations intelligence and knowledge work', *International Symposium on Military Operational Research 2015* (Royal Holloway, University of London, July 2015).

43. McCarthy, *Engineering*, p. 76 (emphasis added); see, historically, as discussed in Jones, *Most Secret War*; and, more recently, as clearly demonstrated in Svendsen, 'Intelligence, surveillance and reconnaissance (ISR)'; A.D.M. Svendsen, 'Sharpening SOF tools, their strategic use and direction', *Defence Studies*, 14, 3 (2014), pp. 284–309; H. Altman, 'New Socom leader Thomas known for broad experience, honest talk', *Tampa Tribune* (30 March 2016); B. Starr, 'U.S. special forces wage secretive "small wars" against terrorists', CNN; M. Vickers, 'Special operations forces: A primary tool', *Cipher Brief* (12/15 May 2016); A. Lysgård, 'The evolution of the global SOF enterprise from a partner perspective', *Joint Special Operations University Occasional Paper* (2016); A. Powell, 'Advice from SOF on the use of SOF for the next administration', *CNA* (2016).

44. See, for instance, as discussed in greater depth in chapter 3.

45. McCarthy, *Engineering*, p. 131; discussed throughout Svendsen, 'Advancing "defence-in-depth"' and Svendsen, 'Contemporary intelligence innovation in practice'.

46. Several sources can be cited here—e.g., A.D.M. Svendsen, 'Advancing system of systems dynamics (SoSD) in the cyber intelligence (CYBINT) domain', *International Society of Military Sciences Conference 2015* (October); D.C. Gompert and M. Libicki, 'Waging cyber war the American way', *Survival*, 57, 4 (2015); K.G. Coleman, 'Cyber: The new no. 1 threat', C4ISRNet; P. Duggan, 'SOF's cyber FRINGE', *Small Wars Journal* (8/10 February 2016); M. Warner, 'Cybersecurity: A pre-history', *Intelligence and National Security*, 27, 5 (2012), pp. 781–99; E. Tikk-Ringas, ed., *Evolution*

of the Cyber Domain (London: IISS, 2015); M.V. Hayden, 'The making of America's cyberweapons', *Christian Science Monitor*; I.R. Porche, III, 'Emerging cyber threats and implications', *Testimony* (Washington, DC: Rand Corporation); J. Siciliano, 'Feds advise utilities to pull plug on Internet after Ukraine attack', *Washington Examiner*, 'Commentary: Putin's options for cyber escalation over Ukraine'; A. Mehta, 'Carter heads to Silicon Valley as ISIS cyberwar expands', *Defense News* (24/25/29 February 2016); C. Young, 'Opinion: Cybersecurity needs less talk, more action', *Christian Science Monitor*, K.G. Coleman, 'Defending the nation's critical infrastructure', *Defense News*; P. Tucker, 'The Ukrainian blackout and the future of war', *Defense One* (4/8/9 March 2016); 'Denmark's intelligence agency creates "hacker academy"', Associated Press; K.G. Coleman, 'Cyber is essential to the "third offset strategy"', C4ISRNet; B.D. Katz, 'U.S. beefs up cyber defenses to thwart hacks of nuclear arsenal', Bloomberg (17/23–24 March 2016); see also 'CLTC Scenarios', Center for Long-term Cybersecurity (Berkeley: University of California Press, 2016); K. Coleman, 'The continuous change of cyber', C4ISRNet (28 July 2016); L. Penn-Hall, 'The blurring line between cyber and physical threats', *Cipher Brief*; C. Wodehouse, 'Trends in cyber security threats and how to prevent them', *B2C* (21/29 August 2016); K. Stoddart, 'UK cyber security and critical national infrastructure protection', *International Affairs*, 92, 5 (2016), pp. 1079–105. With nuclear focus, A.F. Krepinevich, Jr., and J. Cohn, 'Rethinking the apocalypse', *War on the Rocks*; 'Analysis: Don't dismiss, or panic over, N. Korea threats', Associated Press; R. Jeffrey Smith, 'Nuclear security: A vital goal but a distant prospect', Center for Public Integrity, 'Skipping nuclear summit a "missed opportunity" for Russia—White House', Reuters; D.E. Sanger and W.J. Broad, 'Nuclear materials remain vulnerable to theft, despite U.S.–led effort', *New York Times* (1/7/28–29 March 2016); T. Wesolowsky, 'Belarus under fire for "dangerous errors" at nuclear plant', *Guardian* (9 August 2016); R. Rampton and M. Spetalnick, 'Obama: "Madmen" must not be allowed to get nuclear material'; S. Nebehay, 'North Korea to pursue nuclear and missile programmes—Envoy', Reuters; 'North Korea nuclear tests: US and China to co-operate', BBC (1 April 2016); F. Moore, 'North Korea missile test is a game-changing act', *Cipher Brief* (3 August 2016).

47. A. Shtuni, 'Black market supply and demand: The flow of illegal weapons from the Western Balkans to Islamist militants in Western Europe', IHS Jane's 360 (24 March 2016); P. Malone, 'A secret group easily bought the raw ingredients for a dirty bomb—Here in America', Center for Public Integrity (4 August 2016); 'Sweden developing secret ingredient against terrorists', *The Local—Sweden* (25 March 2016). On 'delivery systems' and associated issues, e.g., missile control regimes, see Svendsen, *Understanding the Globalization of Intelligence*, p. 59; M. Weisgerber, 'Pentagon: We're closer than ever to lasers that can stop Iranian, North Korean missiles', *Defense One*; M. Weisgerber, 'The supercomputer that can spot mobile missiles', *Defense One*; 'China expresses concern about Indian missiles on border', Reuters (17–18/25 August 2016); W.J. Broad and D.E. Sanger, 'Race for latest class of nuclear arms threatens to revive Cold War', *New York Times*; D. Ohlbaum, 'US nuclear policy remains dangerously stuck in the past', *The Hill* (16 April/23 August 2016); M. MacCalman, 'A.Q. Khan nuclear smuggling network', *Journal of Strategic Security*, 9, 1 (2016), pp. 104–18; also on the A.Q. Khan network, see Svendsen, *Intelligence*

Cooperation and the War on Terror, p. 33, pp. 103–16; Svendsen, *Understanding the Globalization of Intelligence*, pp. 57–58, pp. 60–62, p. 67, p. 71; Svendsen, *The Professionalization of Intelligence Cooperation*, pp. 140–41; J. Miller, 'Swiss reject man's $1 million damages claim in nuclear bomb secrets case', Reuters; F. Gardner, 'Inside the secret world of explosives forensics', BBC; E. Graham-Harrison, 'Chemical weapons attacks in Syria may normalise war crimes, experts warn', *Guardian*; C. Lynch and D. Kenner, 'U.S. and Europe Say Assad may have kept some chemical weapons', *Foreign Policy*; D. Bryan, 'UN chief calls for renewed focus on mass destruction weapons', Associated Press; J. Judson, 'Hypersonic weapons threat looms large at missile defense symposium', *Defense News*; M. Ravindranath, 'US gets serious about portable nuke-detector prototypes', Nextgov.com (11/17/23 August 2016).

48. McCarthy, *Engineering*, p. 80; refs to 'risk' in Svendsen, 'Advancing "defence-in-depth"', p. 60, p. 61, p. 63, pp. 65–66, p. 67; see also refs to 'risk' and 'resilience' throughout Svendsen, *Understanding the Globalization of Intelligence* and esp. Svendsen, *The Professionalization of Intelligence Cooperation*; more historically, A.D.M. Svendsen, 'Re-fashioning risk', *Defence Studies*, 10, 3 (September 2010), pp. 307–35.

49. McCarthy, *Engineering*, pp. 83–84; on intelligence 'expectations', e.g., Svendsen, *Understanding the Globalization of Intelligence*, p. 129, p. 146; Svendsen, *The Professionalization of Intelligence Cooperation*, p. 43; Svendsen, *Intelligence Cooperation and the War on Terror*, pp. 53–54, p. 85, p. 126, p. 143; J. Lloyd, 'Commentary: Strengthen democracy, hug a spy', Reuters (5 August 2016); on intelligence 'failure(s)', Svendsen, *Understanding the Globalization of Intelligence*, p. 22, p. 52, p. 62, p. 112, p. 114; Svendsen, *The Professionalization of Intelligence Cooperation*, p. 62; Svendsen, *Intelligence Cooperation and the War on Terror*, p. 35, p. 53, p. 58, p. 80, pp. 126–27, pp. 133–35, pp. 147–48, p. 150, p. 152, p. 158; for a seminal article, R.K. Betts, 'Analysis, war; decision: Why intelligence failures are inevitable', *World Politics*, 31, 1 (October 1978), pp. 61–89, see also his *Enemies of Intelligence* (New York: Columbia University Press, 2009); R. Jervis, *Why Intelligence Fails* (Ithaca, NY: Cornell University Press, 2010); J. Rovner, 'Faulty Intelligence', *Foreign Policy* (22 June 2011); and J. Rovner, *Fixing the Facts: National Security and the Politics of Intelligence* (Ithaca, NY: Cornell University Press, 2011).

50. The activities of other intelligence associated 'agents' can similarly be added here, e.g., historically from World War II; M.R.D. Foot, *Six Faces of Courage* (London: Methuen, 1978).

51. McCarthy, *Engineering*, pp. 87–88; Svendsen, *The Professionalization of Intelligence Cooperation*, p. 8, p. 89, p. 91, p. 93, p. 147; Svendsen, *Understanding the Globalization of Intelligence*, p. 107; essays in, inter alia, J. Goldman, ed., *Ethics of Spying* (Lanham, MD: Scarecrow Press, 2005); J. Galliott and W. Reed, eds., *Ethics and the Future of Spying* (London: Routledge, 2016); D.L. Perry, *Ethics in War, Espionage, Covert Action, and Interrogation* (New York: Rowman & Littlefield, 2016 [2nd ed.]); K. Vrist Rønn, 'Intelligence ethics: A critical review and future perspectives', *International Journal of Intelligence and CounterIntelligence*, 29, 4 (2016), pp. 760–84; UK HM Government, 'Data science ethical framework', *Cabinet Office Publication* (19 May 2016); C. Weinbaum, 'Commentary: The ethics

of artificial intelligence in intelligence agencies', Rand Corporation (18 July 2016); N. Bhuta et al., eds., *Autonomous Weapons Systems* (Cambridge: Cambridge University Press, 2016).

52. On intelligence 'best practice(s)', see inter alia, Svendsen, 'Contemporary intelligence innovation in practice', p. 110; for 'standardisation' insights in intelligence contexts, Svendsen, *Understanding the Globalization of Intelligence*, p. 238, col. 1; Svendsen, *The Professionalization of Intelligence Cooperation*, p. 243, col. 2; D. Mützel, 'IATA CEO: "We need global standards on data collection"', EurActiv. com (20 May 2016); R. Tecott and S. Plana, 'Maybe U.S. police aren't militarized enough: Here's what police can learn from soldiers', *Washington Post* (16 August 2016)—also intersects with extent of 'structuredness' and 'hard to softness' of challenges being encountered.

53. McCarthy, *Engineering*, p. 120; Svendsen, *Understanding the Globalization of Intelligence*, p. 24; K. Hicks, 'Keeping America's principles in the age of terrorism', *Defense One* (17 August 2016); on maintaining the 'moral high-ground' advantages, Svendsen, *Intelligence Cooperation and the War on Terror*, pp. 71–72, pp. 92–93, p. 95, p. 99; see also earlier references to different 'levels' of intelligence activities and experience.

54. On 'intelligence and security reach' concepts and for an intelligence 'reach thesis', see, e.g., Svendsen, *Understanding the Globalization of Intelligence*, esp. p. xxi, pp. 109–16; Svendsen, *The Professionalization of Intelligence Cooperation*, pp. 147–49; see also, e.g., T. Owen, 'The NYPD broke its own rules when spying on Muslims, inspector general says', *VICE*; S. Stewart, 'The long arm of Russian intelligence', *Stratfor* (24/25 August 2016); A.D.M. Svendsen, 'Strategy and disproportionality in contemporary conflicts', *Journal of Strategic Studies*, 33, 3 (2010); B. Van Schaack, 'Evaluating proportionality and long-term civilian harm under the laws of war', *Just Security* (29 August 2016).

55. McCarthy, *Engineering*, p. 139 (emphasis added); Svendsen, *The Professionalization of Intelligence Cooperation*, p. 22, p. 155; Svendsen, *Understanding the Globalization of Intelligence*, p. 18, p. 21.

56. See, e.g., Svendsen, *Intelligence Cooperation and the War on Terror*, pp. 98–99; for current 'tasks', 'jobs', and 'requirements' for early 21st century intelligence, see Svendsen, 'Contemporary intelligence innovation in practice', p. 117; 'Seminar: The origins of extremism', Violence Research Centre, University of Cambridge; P. Fabricius, 'Known unknowns and the fight against violent extremism', Institute for Security Studies; E. Viebeck, 'Tony Blair, Leon Panetta to launch antiterrorism commission', *Washington Post*; A.L. Smith, 'Sweden struggles to stop radicalization at home', *Al Jazeera* (17–18/21/23 February 2016); J. Hargreaves, 'Why both sides are wrong in the counter-extremism debate', *The Conversation*; K. Waddell, 'The US government is secretly huddling with tech firms to fight extremism', *Defense One* (3/9 March 2016); J.M. Olsen, 'Swede arrested in Brussels "brainwashed" by militants', Associated Press (10 April 2016); see also the VERA2 project/programme, as cited in chapter 3; refs to 'CONTEST' and 'CONTEST II', the UK's counter-terrorism strategies since 2003—where PREVENT actually forms *only one* pillar of the overall strategy—Svendsen, *Intelligence Cooperation and the War on Terror*, p. 60,

p. 64, p. 93, pp. 98–99; Svendsen, *Understanding the Globalization of Intelligence*, p. 233 col. 2; Svendsen, *The Professionalization of Intelligence Cooperation*, p. 239 col. 1; 'Terror watchdogs express concern about UK extremism plans', Associated Press (9 March 2016); N. Magney, 'CONTEST, prevent: The lessons of UK counterterrorism policy', *Georgetown Security Studies Review* (16 May 2016); C. Nemr, 'Strategies to counter terrorist narratives are more confused than ever', *War on the Rocks* (15 March 2016); 'Ministers "struggle to define extremism"', BBC (22 July 2016); M. Holden, 'Who is an extremist? UK faces legal challenge over strategy to stop radicals', Reuters (17 August 2016); A. Sellers, 'Think global, act local: How to prevent militant extremism at home', German Marshall Fund of the United States; and 'Warriors from the north', *Al Jazeera* (23/31 March 2016); J. Valero, 'EU slow to prioritise fight against radicalisation', *EuroActiv* (4 April 2016); 'Violent extremism mushrooming—UN', News24, 'UN takes on "violent extremism" seen as a cause of terrorism', Associated Press; 'Secretary general calls for NATO to make training a core task for the Alliance in the fight against extremism', NATO; F. Patel and A. Singh, 'The human rights risks of countering violent extremism programs', *Just Security* (6–7 April 2016); M. Piercey, 'Through the looking glass: Harnessing big data to respond to violent extremism', Devex; M. Morell, J.A. 'Sandy' Winnefeld, and S. Vinograd, 'The scourge of extremism: Move beyond the symptoms and treat the disease', *War on the Rocks*; V. Dodd and J. Grierson, 'Revealed: How Anjem Choudary inspired at least 100 British jihadis', *Guardian*; D. Casciani, 'How Anjem Choudary's mouth was finally shut'; 'Anjem Choudary case raises terror law questions', BBC; R. Pantucci, 'Anjem Choudary was a leader: His conviction will damage terror networks', *Guardian* (1/3/16–17 August 2016).

Part II

IMPROVING
INTELLIGENCE ENGINEERING

Chapter Three

The Intelligence and Operations Nexus

BACKGROUND

Intelligence and operations are closely related. They should remain so. However, while that last statement might seem obvious, there are plenty of readily citable examples throughout history where at least elements of disintegration between the two have occurred. Forms of IE performing somewhat of a bridging role have not always been successful. Notably, 'disconnects' or other detrimental conditions and situations have and can quickly develop, such as with so-called intelligence failures becoming evident.[1]

These disconnects occur when the two areas of intelligence and operations are not closely interacting, whether any interaction that is underway is occurring on a harmonious basis or not, and/or through divergent 'wait and watch' (intelligence) or kinetic-ranging 'see and strike' (security/military/law enforcement) approaches and methodologies, employed operationally and/ or strategically.[2] For example, in the policing and law enforcement domain, these episodes occur when 'agreeing on when to share and use intelligence places agencies at loggerheads with each other in times of crisis'. Continuing with the challenges encountered, intelligence-led policing analyst Professor Jerry H. Ratcliffe notes, 'One [agency] wants a terrorist plot to unfold to the fullest extent to advance the investigation and maximise prosecution goals, while the other wants to interrupt the plot as soon as possible and minimise risk'.[3] Goals vary as much as they overlap.

PATHS FORWARD

The purpose of this chapter is to first examine in greater methodological and approach-orientated terms more behind-the-scenes IE-related concepts and tools. These have demonstrable utility when defence (including military), security, and law enforcement (encompassing policing) work occurs during the conduct of multifunctional-to-special operations (MFOs to SOs/SpecOps) across various operational- and battlespaces and during an overall era of globalised strategic risk (GSR).

Simultaneously, all of the GSR-embedded MFOs to SOs/SpecOps unfold while multiplexic situations and conditions of multiplexity prevail. This is where 'multiplex' and its closely associated extended derivatives are defined, beyond their more common cinema usage, as 'involving or consisting of many elements in a complex relationship . . . involving simultaneous transmission of several messages along a single channel of communication'.[4] These highly pluralistic areas are discussed before reaching this chapter's overall conclusions that dovetail the different insights provided.[5]

EMBARKING ON COMPLEX YET NECESSARY JOURNEYS

When discussing Intelligence (#2) and Operations (#3) in this chapter, 'G2' means 'the department of a [military] headquarters responsible for intelligence', while 'J2' means 'the department of a joint headquarters (JHQ) responsible for intelligence'; and 'G3' refers to 'the department of a headquarters responsible for operations and training', while 'J3' signifies 'the department of a joint headquarters (JHQ) responsible for operations and training'.[6]

The intelligence and operations nexus (e.g., G/J2 + G/J3) occurs most clearly and intensively in the technical/technology, collection/gathering, and mission and tactical/operations intelligence to military intelligence (TACINT/OPINT to MILINT/MI) dominating domains of intelligence, surveillance and reconnaissance, frequently known in shorthand either as ISR (ISTAR if target acquisition tasks are included) or as C4ISR if command, control, communications, and computers (C4) considerations are also present.[7] Several different aspects are constantly involved in their juggling.

Worth in-depth evaluation, IE activities provide a consistent seam of continuity between intelligence-related efforts and activities. Particularly, this exploration is undertaken so that farther and higher-reaching, even 'big-picture', synthesis and sense-making, contextualisation, understanding, and knowledge-generation—such as that which relates to broad-ranging intelligence analysis, assessment and estimate efforts and extending to strategic intelligence (STRATINT) and defence intelligence (DEFINT/DI) work—are not underinvested in or overlooked. This is especially necessary in overall strategic and financial or budgeting calculations and in overarching intelligence-related activities and their closely associated domains.[8]

FROM INTELLIGENCE (G/J2)
TO OPERATIONS (G/J3), AND BACK

Intelligence Developments

Taken most basically, #2 intelligence (G/J2) work consists of (1) *collection/ gathering* and (2) *analysis* and *assessment/estimate* activities. Those last activities involve (1) breaking down problems into their differing constitutive components—namely, undertaking analysis tasks and answering *What is it?* queries; and then (2) embarking on assessment/estimate activities, which involve answering *What does it mean? So what?* and *Why?* questions and include the greater synthesis of—at least initial—frameworks and operational parameters for generating situational awareness and fostering broader and deeper conditions of understanding. This knowledge-related work can then be used for helping future decision-making and for framing, viewing, and structuring future activities. These activities include conducting extended investigations and other operations, for instance, for evidence acquisition for use in court, and for further probing any 'secrets' or 'mysteries' that are of interest or concern.[9]

When the above intelligence approaches are adopted in a business-like manner, 'intelligence-led', or 'directed', concepts become increasingly prominent, such as the regularly referenced 'intelligence-led policing'. Intelligence also no longer performs merely its classical, or traditional and conventional, *supporting* role.[10] While they should never be taken uncritically as 'silver bullets'—if only because they are more suggestive in the form and in terms of offering variously scaled 'tips' and 'leads' or, alternatively, providing indicative business models worthy of further exploratory follow-up—the frameworks and operational parameters robustly underpinned and/ or demarcated by intelligence emerge as generally useful guides in several areas. These areas range across familiar leadership and command and control (C2)-related decision-making efforts, and they help formulate, inter alia, areas such as military-associated 'commander intents' for determining and running—extending to advantageously and architecturally designing and shaping through planning—subsequent events and developments, such as consequent investigations, cases, operations, which rules of engagement (RoE) should figure, and so forth.[11]

Operations Insights

The qualities represented by #3 Operations (G/J3) are different. Operations highlight the continued synthesis, implementation, and joining-up of tactics and other 'ways' and 'means' for successfully realising higher-level, more strategic-ranging and desired mission 'ends'.[12] Operations are also where we see IE and its synergistic value emerge with greater clarity, as various tools can be selected from IE-associated toolboxes and toolsets for their subsequent and consequent application or operationalisation through their applied use, as already characterised above. The changes wrought by the conduct of operations directly feed back into the above occurring intelligence (#2) efforts, such as analysis work and the re-evaluative assessment of prevailing situations. This activity is reflected—at least partially—by traditional and classical well-established tools, notably the 'intelligence cycle' model. Ideally, a constantly evolving, iterative process is represented overall.[13]

Ultimately, for intelligence that is applied *during* operations, such as TACINT to OPINT, we do well to (1) maintain the sustained and effective delivery of the intelligence requirements of the '3Rs', which in turn involves 'getting the *right intelligence or information*, to the *right person or people*, at the *right time*'; and (2) continue to simultaneously meet and consistently maintain over time all of the highly pressing customer and end-user intelligence-delivery criteria relating to specificity, timeliness, accuracy, relevance and clarity (STARC).[14]

As noted, these efforts are undertaken in highly complex contexts while intelligence practitioners and other involved operatives strive to navigate the huge array of demands and 'mission-creep', even 'mission-gallop', generated by negotiating the conduct of several multifunctional and special operations (MFOs-SOs/SpecOps). In their entirety, these operations cover a range of activities from war to peace, which includes dealing with a full spectrum of diverse concerns such as crisis management, peacekeeping, disaster-response and humanitarian operations, cyber, counter-insurgency (COIN), counter-terrorism (CT), counter-proliferation (CP), the countering of transnational serious organised crimes, the countering of human, drugs, and narcotics trafficking, and more. Meanwhile, all of the above MFOs and SOs/SpecOps occur both in and across the five closely interconnected physical (sea, air, land, space) and virtual (cyber) domains and over many different timeframes and timelines. MFOs and SOs/SpecOps also occur during an overall era of globalised strategic risk (GSR) while prevailing multiplexic events and developments are simultaneously unfolding in 'complex co-existence plurality' (CCP) environments.[15]

EXTENDED IE CONSIDERATIONS

Circumstances set frames and tempos. A constant loop and feedback process of 'context appreciation'—otherwise known as contexualisation—*and* 'solution fashioning'—or trouble-shooting to problem-solving—thus emerges as important. This closely interacting and iterative process should be kept in mind and applied at all times.[16]

IE and its associated tools, toolboxes, and toolsets essentially provide the 'pivot' around which the above activities can cluster, reinforcing its importance.[17] At its most basic, IE assists as an appropriate tool-selector for those nuanced circumstances encountered and experienced where 'a sledgehammer may be great for laying train rails, but you need to recognise that it won't be very good for hammering finishing nails on a picture frame'.[18]

IE NAVIGATING VIA 'SYSTEMS' TO 'SYSTEM OF SYSTEMS DYNAMICS' (SOSD)

The 'intelligence and operations nexus' (#2 + #3 or G/J2 + G/J3) can be bridged in several ways. As suggested in chapter 2, many of the elements employed will be immediately familiar to engineers or indeed to anyone with even a general understanding of engineering. This observation underlines where IE emerges as a useful tool for further refinement both now and for the future, and as advanced by intelligence and other security and defence practitioners, including those operators involved in crisis and emergency management to civil-protection activities. Business sector managers and other enterprise managers can similarly benefit because of the intimately involved flows of critical information.

A GUIDE TO IE

In this discussion of IE, *multilevel* approaches are first drawn on, as illustrated in figure 3.1. These approaches involve

> eight different, yet interrelated, levels of activity and experience. They each offer many different insights, and can hence be subsequently used for analysis purposes. Ranging from 'high' and 'macro' to 'low' and 'micro', these levels comprise: (i) the ideological level; (ii) the theoretical level; (iii) the strategy

Where to go next? #3

- + inc. covering **8x levels of (inter-)activity/implementation**:

CHECKLIST

1. Ideological
2. Theoretical
3. Strategic
4. Policy
5. Operational
6. Tactical
7. Individual (as 'professional')
8. Personal

UNDERSTANDING THE GLOBALIZATION OF INTELLIGENCE — ADAM D.M. SVENDSEN

THE PROFESSIONALIZATION OF INTELLIGENCE COOPERATION — FASHIONING METHOD OUT OF MAYHEM — ADAM D.M. SVENDSEN

- + **'Reach' concepts** >>> **'under-reach'** + **'over-reach'**

- Need realise **'optimised reach balance(s)'** in overall enterprises

- (cf. A.D.M. Svendsen (2012), *Understanding the Globalization of Intelligence*, e.g. p.12, etc. + A.D.M. Svendsen (2012), *The Professionalization of Intelligence Cooperation*.)

Figure 3.1. Levels
Courtesy of the Author

level; (iv) the policy level; (v) the operational level; (vi) the tactical level; (vii) the individual (as 'professional') level; and (viii) the personal level.[19]

Second, *systems* are highlighted. Since many systems prevail in relation to intelligence, as is often argued, we need to further and better harness them in intelligence contexts and with regard to a wide range of intelligence phenomena, such as during intelligence analysis and subsequent intelligence-engineering efforts.[20] As previous research elsewhere on the more specific and technical phenomenon of 'intelligence liaison' (intelligence cooperation) has already identified at length—with wide applicability for being harnessed more generally in relation to other intelligence phenomena—eight basic, interacting system attributes or variables can be identified as constitutive event and development 'building-blocks', and these can have a transformative impact when so managed. In turn, the eight system attributes or variables consist of

1. internal influences/factors
2. rationale

3. types and forms
4. conditions and terms
5. trends
6. functions
7. external influences/factors
8. effects and outcomes (see figure 3.2)[21]

In intelligence enterprises, for practitioners and operators, these system variables or attributes boast the benefit of being employable as indicators in a checklist manner. They can also be deployed in a pre-flight–style mode, as suggested during both (1) analysis and (2) subsequent engineering activities.[22]

Third, '*federation* or *System of Systems*' (SoS) and all of its associated dynamics (SoSD) are referenced. As illustrated in figure 3.3, during the course of engaging in System of Systems Analysis or SoSA work, many different dimensions come to the fore, together with examples of many different organisations, such as the North Atlantic Treaty Organisation (NATO), the European Police Office (EUROPOL), and the U.S. Military, all using variants of these SoSA tools in the different operational- and battlespaces in which they

Where to go next? #2

- That last **SoSD model** inc. covering **8x systemic attributes or variables**:

CHECKLIST

1. internal influences/factors;
2. rationale;
3. types and forms;
4. conditions and terms;
5. trends;
6. functions;
7. external influences/factors; +
8. effects and outcomes.

- (cf. A.D.M. Svendsen (2012), *Understanding the Globalization of Intelligence*, pp.99-107)

Figure 3.2. System attributes or variables
Courtesy of the Author

Where we are today #1

- Currently **use/rely on SoSA** approaches, breaking-down 'problems' in op. spaces into readily graspable dimensions of, e.g.:

  - **'PMESII'** ('Political, Military, Economic, Social, Informational and Infrastructural'), e.g. used by NATO;

  - **'PESTLE'** (Political, Economic, Sociological/Social, Technological/ Technology, Legal/Legislative, Environmental), e.g. used by EUROPOL;

  - **'DIME'** (Diplomatic, Information, Military, Economic);

  - **'HSCB'** (Human, Social, Cultural, Behavioural), e.g. as both used by US Military;

  - **'STEEP(L)'** (Social, Technology, Economic, Environmental, Political, [Legal]), e.g. as used in commercial/business intelligence contexts, etc.

Figure 3.3.   System of Systems Dynamics (SoSD)
Courtesy of the Author

work and have to engage.[23] Several important actors, both civilian and military (CIV/MIL) and policy- to decision-makers and other operatives (POL/ MIL) clearly benefit from the harnessing of these SoSD tools and equally from an improved understanding of them.[24]

LINKING BACK TO G/J2-G/J3 WORK

More fundamentally, SoSA aspects particularly closely overlap with #2 and G/J2 Intelligence considerations. Furthermore, when taken most fully into account, SoSA work appropriately captures the 'M4IS2: multiagency, multinational, multidisciplinary, multidomain information sharing and sense making' activities, which range across the 'eight entities [of] commerce, academic, government, civil society, media, law enforcement, military and non-government/non-profit', as identified by security analyst Glen Segell, amongst others.[25]

Equally, embarking on SoSA work further underlines the demonstrable importance both of and more actively 'doing' increasingly diverse intelligence work to its fullest. This includes open source intelligence/information (OSINT/OSINF) endeavours, together with related social media intelligence (SOCMINT) and research-originating material intelligence, or RESINT, work, as well as seizing—still continuing to rapidly develop and evolve— collective intelligence, or COLINT, paradigms. These are taken as part of 'all-source' or 'multi-INTs' (multiple intelligence disciplines) work.[26] As already seen, cyber intelligence (CYBINT) considerations are similarly significant.[27] All of these differing dimensions should not be overlooked either in whole or part.

Operational (#3 and G/J3) aspects then figure more explicitly. Hand-in-glove with wider IE efforts, these unfold during System of Systems Engineering (SoSE) work, which occurs in tandem with and once SoSA and the stronger #2 Intelligence (e.g., G/J2) activities have been undertaken.[28] The main focus during the course of SoSE involves more synthesis and building tasks, as well as developing connective-oriented activities (joining the dots).

Collectively underpinned by IE and involving both SoSA and SoSE efforts, overall System of Systems Dynamics (SoSD) approaches and methodologies have a broad scope. They extend across #2 Intelligence and #3 Operations (e.g., G/J2 + G/J3) domains with much evident applicable utility.[29] Many combinations persist and, most ideally, should continue to do so.

HOW TO PUT IT ALL TOGETHER?
IE RELEVANT SOSD IN ACTION

Fusion activities now form the main focus for IE. Once we have identified all of the different components involved—with (1) codification of the multiple levels, (2) detailing of the system variables and attributes, and (3) a demonstration of the different System of Systems Dynamics (SoSD) dimensions— the question of how to put it all together next emerges prominently.

During at least operational and architectural design and planning processes, effective ways forward are to draw on a series of well-established— and therefore already highly familiar (due to their widespread adoption)— issue-problem-hazard-risk and up to threat grid-mapping techniques and tools.[30] Along with the logical rationales for their use, these evaluative grids, tables, or matrices are illustrated in figures 3.4–3.9[31] together with two mini case-study examples of their use in relation to evaluating the current intelligence concern and target of the Islamic State, or IS/ISIS/ISIL/Da'esh, both (1) generally (figure 3.5); and (2) with more of a specific cyber intelligence (CYBINT) focus (figure 3.6).[32] (See also the uncompleted IE mapping templates in the appendix.)

How to put it all together? #1

Overall 'Situational Awareness' Evaluation (SoSA/G-J2)
CONTEXT APPRECIATION - Observe + Orient

System attributes/ variables > e.g. inc. captures + covers...? > SoSA units (e.g. PMESII):	Internal influences / factors 'Who?' / 'Which?'	Rationale 'Why?'	Types + Forms 'What?'	Conditions + Terms 'When?'	Trends (+ dynamics/ flows) 'Where?'	Functions 'How?'	External influences / factors 'Who?' / 'Which?'	Effects + Outcomes 'What?' / 'S.W.O.T.'
Political (inc. law/legislation)								
Military								
Economic								
Social (inc. sociological + cultural)								
Informational/ Intelligence (inc. technological)								
Infrastructural (inc. environment[al])								

This matrix is designed to provide an analytic framework with **core - even checkbox - criteria or variables to consider** into which evaluators can record as holistically as possible - e.g., through mapping - what they observe from, e.g., a selected case/issue/problem, etc.

This approach enables the **comprehensive capturing** of - if not all - at least several different aspects of an event/episode, issue, etc., in its **varying key dimensions.**

Figure 3.4.   Fusion Matrix/Table/Grid Map #1
Courtesy of the Author

An example of fusion: ISIS

Overall 'Situational Awareness' Evaluation (SoSA/G-J2)
CONTEXT APPRECIATION - Observe + Orient

System attributes/ variables > e.g. inc. captures + covers...? > SoSA units (e.g. PMESII):	Internal influences / factors 'Who?' / 'Which?'	Rationale 'Why?'	Types + Forms 'What?'	Conditions + Terms 'When?'	Trends (+ dynamics/ flows) 'Where?'	Functions 'How?'	External influences / factors 'Who?' / 'Which?'	Effects + Outcomes 'What?' / 'S.W.O.T.'
Political (inc. law/legislation)	Sharia law / alternative hierarchies	Unrep. elsewhere/ power-play	Strong leadership	Fill governance vacuum	Exploiting Iraq/Syria weaknesses	Ruthless / kill off opposition	Sympathisers	Imposing regime
Military	Tight, well-disciplined C2	Got weapons / tactics	e.g. Heavy +automatic weaponry	Succeed vs. weaker/ disorg. oppo	Good at capturing; less so at holding?	Agile / flexible / fast-lightfoot	Ex-military personnel	Competent committed adversary
Economic	Profitable/ employed	Make profit - e.g. oil	Steady supply funding	Exploit existing/new markets	Exploiting oil-refineries	Able to sell, e.g. oil	Resp to consumer demands	Self-sustaining/ autarky?
Social (inc. sociological + cultural)	Camarad-erie/ purpose	Romance	Bonding/ band-bros/ marriage	Links/ties - e.g. friends/ passions	Native + Foreign fighters	Quasi-religious/ smashing activities	'Call of the wild'/ share adventurism	Soft + not just hard factors
Informational/ Intelligence (inc. technological)	Good / soc media / BYOD	Able to influence	Social media/ propaganda	INFO/ PSYOPS = work	Use internet - e.g. Twitter	Access to electronic devices	Acquiescence support thru intimidation	Shifting frames of reference
Infrastructural (inc. environment[al])	Good networks/ comms	Can seize/ control/ trade/nego	Training camps/bases	Using what is there - e.g. roads...	Urban/settled/ travel-able areas	Travel on roads / oil refinery use	Unwitting(?) private service prov	Too depend on what have already?

Figure 3.5.   Fusion Example: Islamic State.   IS/ISIS/ISIL/Da'esh
Courtesy of the Author

CYBINT ANALYSIS INSIGHTS FUSION EXAMPLE: ISIS

Overall 'Situational Awareness' Evaluation (SoSA/G-J2)
CONTEXT APPRECIATION - Observe + Orient

System attributes/ variables > e.g. inc. captures + covers...? > SoSA units (e.g. PMESII):	Internal influences / factors 'Who?' / 'Which?'	Rationale 'Why?'	Types + Forms 'What?'	Conditions + Terms 'When?'	Trends (+ dynamics/ flows) 'Where?'	Functions 'How?'	External influences / factors 'Who?' / 'Which?'	Effects + Outcomes 'What?' / 'S.W.O.T.'
Political (inc. law/legislation)	Sharia law / alternative hierarchies	Unrep. elsewhere/ power-play	Strong leadership	Fill governance vacuum	Exploiting Iraq/Syria weaknesses	Ruthless / kill off opposition	Sympathis ers	Imposing regime
Military	Tight, well-disciplined C2	Got weapons / tactics	e.g. Heavy +automatic weaponry	Succeed vs. weaker/ disorg. oppo	Good at capturing; less so at holding?	Agile / flexible / fast-lightfoot	Ex-military personnel	Competent committed adversary
Economic	Profitable/ employed	Make profit - e.g. oil	Steady supply funding	Exploit existing/new markets	Exploiting oil-refineries	Able to sell, e.g. oil	Resp to consumer demands	Self-sustaining/ autarky?
Social (inc. sociological + cultural)	Camarad -erie/ purpose	Romance	Bonding/ band-bros/ marriage	Links/ties - e.g. friends/ passions	Native + Foreign fighters	Quasi-religious/ smashing activities	'Call of the wild'/ share adventurism	Soft + not just hard factors
Informational/ Intelligence (inc. technological)	Good / soc media = BYOD	Able to influence	Social media/ propaganda	INFO/ PSYOPS = work	Use internet - e.g. Twitter	Access to electronic devices	Acquiescence support thru intimidation	Shifting frames of reference
Infrastructural (inc. environment[al])	Good networks/ comms	Can seize/ control/ trade/nego	Training camps/bases	Using what is there - e.g. roads...	Urban/settled/ travel-able areas	Travel on roads / oil refinery use	Unwitting(?) private service prov	Too depend on what have already!

N.B.: main CYBINT concerns **not isolated from the other aspects** encounter + need to consider more widely

Figure 3.6. Fusion Example: Cyber Intelligence (CYBINT)
Courtesy of the Author

How to put it all together? #2

Overall 'Mission Accomplishment' Guide (SoSE/G-J3)
SOLUTION FASHIONING - Decide + Act

SoSA units (e.g. PMESII) > 'Levels' (of interactivity/ implementation/ engineering):	Political (inc. law/legislation)	Military	Economic	Social (inc. sociological + cultural)	Informational/ Intelligence (inc. technological)	Infrastructural (inc. environment[al])
Ideological (e.g. Ideas/Why realise?)						
Theoretical (e.g. Aspirations/Why do?)						
Strategic (e.g. Directions/How go?)						
Policy (e.g. Aims/Where go?)						
Operational (e.g. How/What realise?)						
Tactical (e.g. How/What do?)						
Individual (as 'professional') (e.g. What/Which realise?)						
Personal (e.g. Who do?)						

Deliverable work filling/completing this matrix (+ the one given on prev. slide) can be **done 'live'** - e.g. in a real battlespace/operational context ('pre-flight' style); or equally can be **done more 'off-line'** + in the abstract - e.g. during a simulation/training/exercise in the classroom.

Overall, these **matrices form useful analytical frameworks + educational teaching tools**, also helping to advance standards + best practices in approaches towards situation evaluations + subsequent transformation.

Also suggests **where 'to draw the line'** in relation to issues, e.g. privacy, etc.

Privacy buffer

Figure 3.7. Fusion Matrix/Table/Grid Map #2
Courtesy of the Author

The inputs, and hence the insights, presented in and communicated by the examples cited above (figures 3.5 and 3.6) are then ready to be imported as outputs for use as inputs in the next grid map, map 2 (see figure 3.7). This is for use in (1) 'online' and 'real-time', or 'actual' and 'live', operational and battlespace circumstances as well as in (2) 'off-line' training and war-gaming simulation—for example, during workshops.[33]

With this overall approach, clear guidance is also offered as to where 'privacy-by-design'–influenced safeguards feature. This work includes conducting privacy impact assessments (PIAs) and implementing other privacy-addressing concerns. For instance, these figure in the form of locating where an explicitly drawn, protective, 'privacy-buffer' line can be inserted in overall intelligence-related systems during the course of progressing, multilevel defence and security enterprises. Implementing existing and developing bodies of management, business, and IT enterprise–related standards and best practices similarly boasts overarching value.[34]

Using another grid, as represented by map 3 (see figure 3.8), work for fostering greater understanding and for further knowledge-generation-to-testing purposes is then engaged.

How to put it all together? #3

Fusion grid = mapping System Attributes/Variables + Levels
for each specified SoS unit of analysis* - e.g. using PMESII model: Political; Military;
Economic; Social; Informational/Intelligence; Infrastructural (*show which is selected for focus)

System Attributes/ Variables> ---------- 'Levels' (of interactivity/ implementation/ engineering):	Internal influences / factors 'Who?' / 'Which?'	Rationale 'Why?'	Types + Forms 'What?'	Conditions + Terms 'When?'	Trends (+ dynamics/ flows) 'Where?'	Functions 'How?'	External influences / factors 'Who?' / 'Which?'	Effects + Outcomes 'What?' / 'S.W.O.T.'
Ideological (e.g. Ideas/Why realise?)								
Theoretical (e.g. Aspirations/Why do?)								
Strategic (e.g. Directions/How go?)								
Policy (e.g. Aims/Where go?)								
Operational (e.g. How/What realise?)								
Tactical (e.g. How/What do?)								
Individual (as 'professional') (e.g. What/Which realise?)								Privacy buffer
Personal (e.g. Who do?)								

This third chart (table) for mapping allows for 'triangulation' to be undertaken, e.g. with the results from the other two previous charts, during overall 'fusion' activities.

Figure 3.8. Fusion Matrix/Table/Grid Map #3
Courtesy of the Author

Once the rich wealth of insights presented in maps 1–3 has been demonstrated in their completion and display, a greater rationalisation or concentration of their distilled insights proves helpful. We accomplish this distilling by focusing on three areas central to events and developments, namely (1) key actors, (2) forces/factors of change, and (3) possible change over time—while simultaneously providing what can be characterised as an 'operational picture' overview relating to a fusion of the above three core considerations (see figure 3.9).[35]

The fusion of the three core considerations (however precisely scaled) allows for a more informed fashioning of overarching 'signifier nodes', which reflect the overall 'operational picture' and what it communicates. These signifier nodes can then be taken for positioning on tailor-made, triage-related, traffic-light colour-coded SoSD–based, or oriented, 'indicator boards'. These indicator boards use the conventional prioritisation-related mechanisms of red for 'alert', amber for 'warning', and green for 'be aware', including enough scope for incorporating quantifiable probability scorings—for example, represented as percentages relating to occurrence likelihood.[36]

Advanced Intelligence Analysis + Engineering - AIAE
Mapping Sheet #4

OVERVIEW SNAPSHOT SUMMARY
At a minimum for context consider + fuse:

(A) 'Key Actors' - e.g. who? (e.g. OC groups, individuals, other 'targets', etc.)	**(A1) Events** - e.g. what? when? where?
	(A2) Patterns - e.g. how?
	(A3) Drivers - e.g. why?
(B) 'forces/factors of change' - e.g. what activity? (e.g. SOC areas, etc.)	**(B1) Events** - e.g. what? when? where?
	(B2) Patterns - e.g. how?
	(B3) Drivers - e.g. why?
(C) 'possible change over time' - e.g. when? / where? (e.g. environment, PESTLE/PMESII [SoSD] indicators, SWOT, etc.)	**(C1) Events** - e.g. what? when? where?
	(C2) Patterns - e.g. how?
	(C3) Drivers - e.g. why?

Aim = capture: (i) the **players**; (ii) their **relationships**; (iii) their **drivers** (e.g. their **means, motives & opportunities**). Adam D.M. Svendsen, PhD

Figure 3.9. Fusion Matrix/Table/Grid Map #4
Courtesy of the Author

EXTENDED INSIGHTS

By adopting the combination of approaches sketched above, much is readied for tasks such as the provision of insights that range differently across varying factors (e.g., those relating to diverse geostrategic landscapes) and differing timeframes or lines (temporally). These varying approaches and their fusion will also be helpful for generating greater strategic-relevant 'context appreciation' (or contextualisation) and enhanced 'situational awareness' extending to deeper and wider conditions of knowledge and understanding. Those outcomes, in turn, offer a further array of advanced insights which help contribute towards assisting us in making *Where next?* and other associated response decisions.[37] This forward-looking approach and horizon-scanning method also boasts greater strategic early warning (SEW) potential, including for generating enhanced foresight.

CONCLUSIONS

IE figures centrally and performs a key role in the intelligence and operations nexus. As demonstrated in this chapter, IE activities, via the use of (1) multilevel approaches (including eight different, identified levels of experience and activities) which, in turn, are then valuable for analysis and engineering purposes; (2) systems (including their eight different, systematic attributes and variables); and (3) System of Systems Dynamics (SoSD)—including PMESII, PESTLE, DIME, HSCB, STEEP(L), etc., of SoSA and SoSE activities—all help provide the ways and means of navigating and negotiating the #2 Intelligence to #3 Operations relationships. These #2 and #3 (G/J2 + G/J3) relationships, in turn, then cohere and connect in a constant, feedback-looping interaction for the overarching intent of heading in the direction of accomplishing desired operational and strategic ends. Morphing and updating as they go onwards or run forward, several joining up, IE-related activities emerge. When harnessing the (semi-)structured techniques provided via the evaluative grids, we simultaneously keep in place sufficiently fixed variable controls. IE references and referrals remain in a suitably enduring manner without shifting out of focus or perspective or eluding their later re-capture or recall.

FROM THEORY TO PRACTICE AND BACK

The engineering-associated efforts overall encompassed by IE activities help bring theories and ideas, aims and intents, into practice and action. This proactive work includes realising operational designs and plans through embarking on next steps, notably the implementation of those blueprints. As seen, thinking in strong management, business, and IT *enterprise* terms, such as by drawing on standards and their attendant standardisation processes, by introducing best practices, and so forth, emerges as valuable to the full spectrum of security and defence practitioners. This includes anyone intimately involved in any form of intelligence or critical information–related work', such as crisis managers and emergency planners. Their safety-related work can be further articulated, even augmented, via related developing areas, most notably evolving business-process modelling and management (BPM) approaches.[38]

When engaging in IE, the SoSD referenced throughout this chapter and employed as illustrated in figures 3.1–3.9 can clearly be used both (1) generally in overarching intelligence, defence, security, and law enforcement enterprises—as the case relating to the Islamic State (IS/ISIL/ISIS/Da'esh) demonstrates; as well as (2) more specifically, such as highlighted in the cyber intelligence (CYBINT) mini case-study example and as particularly shown in figure 3.6. This allows us more advanced ways for better facilitating and generating enhanced insights into sophisticated areas, such as conducting more expansive strategic futures work, helping structure and develop scenarios, guiding intelligence liaison relationships, and so on.[39]

Arguably, the IE-based SoSA + SoSE or SoSD approach advanced throughout this chapter better (1) captures 'intelligence dynamics'—such as information flows, cybernetic 'feedback-loop', networked dimensions, and so on—that are often found in, inter alia, military and special operations knowledge and practical work as well as mainstream business sector work; (2) joins the many different systems that are involved and encountered during MFOs-to-SOs/SpecOps in overall GSR, CCP, and multiplexic environments; (3) fills any gaps experienced or encountered—or at least pinpoints them by identifying more clearly where persisting gaps or differently ranging unknowns might be, especially where specific grid-map boxes cannot be filled in or completed and when they act indicatively as 'tips' and 'leads' requiring diligent follow-up or further exploration (e.g., relating to 'known-unknowns'); and (4) offers greater contextualisation of—for instance—human geography and sociocultural, knowledge-related, full-spectrum issues, problems, hazards, risks, and threats.[40] The IE framework therefore extends far.

IE WAYS, MEANS, AND ENDS

Advancing integrated, comprehensive SoSA + SoSE or SoSD approaches furthermore assists in the meeting of 'mission accomplishment' ends. These efforts include helping to transform whatever is unfolding and better keeping ahead of the prevailing curve of events and developments.[41] Equally, SoSD approaches can (1) be readily overlaid with other—perhaps more familiar— approaches, such as John Boyd's OODA Loop of observe, orient, decide, and act; (2) help ensure sustained delivery of the 3Rs and the meeting of STARC requirements (as introduced above); (3) encourage greater essential 'thinking outside of the box' in general defence and security as well as more specific military and special operations intelligence and knowledge work missions; and (4) offer further assistance in and with both collection and analysis during the progression of overall intelligence enterprises, including better refining IS(TA)R platforms' foci, tasking, and targeting, and so on, also paying close attention to both hardware and software considerations (for instance, relating to their continued optimisation).[42]

THINKING BIG AND BEING VISIONARY

Ultimately grander, IE-related strategic, architectural, design, and shaping approaches are especially pressing. This is particularly true (1) in our contemporary 'Big Data' and 'Cyber' age;[43] (2) under conditions of 'sensory'—for instance, IS(TA)R-platform—and 'information/data' overload—often, somewhat paradoxically, with coverage shortcomings;[44] (3) as more collective intelligence (COLINT) work is undertaken while at the same time receiving greater public scrutiny (whether welcome or not, and including the careful handling and vetting of so-called Good Samaritans and their well-meant contributions to crisis situations);[45] (4) while intelligence-related defence and security enterprises are continually subject to, for example, Snowden-related so-called revelations and all the associated, even manufactured or manipulated, mistrust and distrust they bring with them;[46] and (5) as related and challenging 'legalisation' or 'legalism' trends continue to extend increasingly into intelligence and investigative domains, necessitating 'smart law' and its greater engagement and encouragement, including better weighing 'soft' and 'hard law' dimensions.[47] Because rapidly made 'deal', 'capture', and 'kill' (or so-called kill-chain associated) decisions frequently figure, creative IE remains critical, especially while decisions are being made on several a priori to post facto bases, meaning that they will unfold either ahead of or behind the curve of events and developments in highly multiplexic circumstances.[48]

In the next chapter, a step-by-step process is proposed for helping navigate risk and for better negotiating overall uncertainty.

NOTES

1. See, e.g., chapter 2; J.J. Wirtz, *Understanding Intelligence Failure* (London: Routledge, 2016); E.J. Dahl, *Intelligence and Surprise Attack* (Washington, DC: Georgetown University Press, 2013); P. Dixon, 'How to predict the future? Look to the past', *Wired* (7 June 2016); C. Andrew, 'Intelligence analysis needs to look backwards before looking forward', History and Policy (1 June 2004); J. Guldi and D. Armitage, *The History Manifesto* (Cambridge: Cambridge University Press, 2014 [2015]); G. Allison and N. Ferguson, 'Why the U.S. president needs a council of historians', *Atlantic* (September 2016); J. Tarabay, 'To defeat future terrorists, Europe must look to the past', *Defense One*; 'The lasting legacy of Sayyid Qutb', Soufan Group (14/29 August 2016); A.D.M. Svendsen, *Understanding the Globalization of Intelligence* (Basingstoke, UK: Palgrave Macmillan, 2012), p. 103; H.I. Ansoff, 'Managing strategic surprise by response to weak signals', *California Management Review*, 18, 2 (1975), pp. 21–33; N. Silver, *The Signal and the Noise* (London: Allen Lane, 2012).

2. See, e.g., refs to 'intelligence failure(s)' in chapter 2; see also different operational approaches and methods in A.D.M. Svendsen, *Intelligence Cooperation and the War on Terror* (London: Routledge, 2010), esp., p. 34, p. 43; A.D.M. Svendsen, 'The Federal Bureau of Investigation and change', *Intelligence and National Security*, 27, 3 (June 2012), esp. p. 393; H. Samuel, 'Syrian moderate rebel "spymaster" slams CIA for "ignoring" detailed intel on Isil since 2013', *Daily Telegraph* (15 March 2016); associated debates, in, inter alia, J. Dorschner, 'In search of an ISR/strike bargain', IHS Jane's 360 (2014); H. Williams, 'Strike out: Unmanned systems set for wider attack role'; M. Malenic, 'UCLASS: Surveillance or strike?' IHS Jane's 360 (2015); H. Peake, 'Special: A spectrum of views on the use of drones', *CSI*, 59, 4 (December 2015); M.V. Hayden, 'To keep America safe, embrace drone warfare', *New York Times*; M. Zenko, 'Michael Hayden's defense of drone warfare doesn't add up', *Defense One* (19/21 February 2016); H. Neidig, 'White House to release drone "playbook"', *The Hill*; G. Packer, 'Can you keep a secret?' *New Yorker*, G. Jennings, 'UK outlines extent of Reaper UAV strikes in Iraq and Syria', IHS Jane's 360; D. Ollivant and M. Hersh, 'A more granular look at death by drone', *War on the Rocks* (5/7/24/29 March 2016); 'Drone: Inside the CIA's secret drone war', *Al Jazeera*; C. Kennedy-Pipe et al., 'Drone chic', *ISN/ETHZ/ORG* (3 April 2016); 'Obama administration releases redacted version of drone policy', Reuters; D. Cole, 'The drone presidency', *New York Review of Books*; J.L. Hazelton, 'The political role of drone strikes in US grand strategy', *The Conversation* (6/17–18 August 2016).

3. J.H. Ratcliffe, *Intelligence-Led Policing* (London: Routledge, 2016 [2 ed.]), p. 187; see also in A.D.M. Svendsen, 'On "a continuum with expansion"? Intelligence co-operation in Europe in the early twenty-first century', in C. Kaunert and S. Leonard, eds., *European Security, Terrorism, and Intelligence* (Basingstoke, UK: Palgrave Macmillan, 2013), p. 185; B. Fägersten, 'For EU eyes only? Intelligence and European security', *EUISS Issue Brief 8* (March 2016); M. Atkinson, 'Dutch Islamic groups resist becoming informers in surveillance drive', *Middle East Eye*;

R. Macmillan, 'Canadian police say man in Ontario raid was in final stages of attack plan', Reuters (8/11 August 2016); A.D.M. Svendsen, 'Re-fashioning risk', *Defence Studies*, 10, 3 (September 2010), esp. pp. 323–25.

4. Definition of 'multiplex' from *Oxford Dictionary of English* (2015); for use of 'multiplex world' concepts, J. Kirkpatrick, 'Interview—Amitav Acharya', E-International Relations (April 2016); 'Criminal Intelligence Coordinating Council (CICC) helps law enforcement share information and intelligence to prevent crime and terrorism', *ISE Bulletin* (3 April 2016); see also T. Bukkvoll, 'Russian special operations forces in Crimea and Donbas', *Parameters*, 46, 2 (2016), pp. 13–21.

5. See these contemporary operating environments as characterised in, inter alia, A.D.M. Svendsen, 'Advancing "defence-in-depth"', *Defense & Security Analysis*, 31, 1 (2015), esp. p. 58 and p. 67; W. Laverick, *Global Injustice and Crime Control* (London: Routledge, 2016); P. O'Malley, 'Revisiting the classics: "Policing the Risk Society" in the twenty-first century', *Policing and Society*, 25, 4 (2015), pp. 426–31; Svendsen, 'The Federal Bureau of Investigation and change', pp. 371–97; D.E. Tromblay, 'The threat review and prioritization trap', *Intelligence and National Security* (2015); J. Warren, 'Special ops rule in war on terror', *The Daily Beast*; M. Nippert, 'Spies and soldiers big budget winners', *NZ Herald* (28–29 May 2016); W. Young and D. Stebbins, 'A rapidly changing urban environment', Rand Corporation (2016).

6. R. Bowyer, *Campaign Dictionary of Military Terms* (Oxford: Macmillan, 2004 [3 ed.]), p. 104 and p. 131.

7. See as discussed in-depth throughout A.D.M. Svendsen, 'Intelligence, surveillance and reconnaissance (ISR)', in J. Deni and D. Galbreath, eds., *The Routledge Handbook of Defence Studies* (London: Routledge, forthcoming); 'B.A.H. sponsored: Collaboration at acquisition yields long-term C4ISR success', *Defense One* (30 March 2016).

8. See also G.F. Treverton and T.M. Sanderson, 'Strategic intelligence: A view from the National Intelligence Council (NIC)', Center for Strategic and International Studies (Washington, DC: 4 March 2016); P.B. Symon and A. Tarapore, 'Defense intelligence analysis in the age of big data', *Joint Forces Quarterly*, 79 (Q4 2015), pp. 4–11; E. Pecht and A. Tishler, 'Budget allocation, national security, military intelligence; human capital: A dynamic model', *Defence and Peace Economics* (November 2015); A. Sternstein, 'There's a big loophole in the Pentagon's guide to eavesdropping', Nextgov.com (19 August 2016).

9. For further detailed insights, Svendsen, *Understanding the Globalization of Intelligence*, p. 5; A.D.M. Svendsen, *The Professionalization of Intelligence Cooperation* (Basingstoke, UK: Palgrave Macmillan, 2012), p. 143, p. 150; A. Sambei, 'Intelligence cooperation versus evidence collection and dissemination', chapter 7 in L. van den Herik and N. Schrijver, eds., *Counter-terrorism Strategies in a Fragmented International Legal Order* (Cambridge: Cambridge University Press, 2013), pp. 212–39. For a range of in-depth informing 'structured analytic techniques' useful for intelligence analysis, strategic futures work, and for helping decision-making, e.g., via its greater support, see as detailed throughout R.J. Heuer, Jr. and R.H. Pherson, *Structured Analytic Techniques for Intelligence Analysis* (Washington, DC: CQ Press, 2014 [2 ed.]).

10. Svendsen, *Understanding the Globalization of Intelligence*, p. 82; Svendsen, *The Professionalization of Intelligence Cooperation*, p. 6; A. James, *Examining Intelligence-Led Policing* (Basingstoke, UK: Palgrave Macmillan, 2013); R. Sinclair Cotter, 'Police intelligence: Connecting-the-dots in a network society', *Policing and Society* (June 2015); A. James, *Understanding Police Intelligence Work* (Bristol: Policy Press, 2016); Ratcliffe, *Intelligence-Led Policing*.

11. See refs to 'intelligence' in R. Smith, *The Utility of Force* (London: Penguin, 2006); R.Z. George, 'Intelligence and strategy', chapter 8 in J. Baylis, J.J. Wirtz, and C.S. Gray, eds., *Strategy in the Contemporary World* (Oxford: Oxford University Press, 2016 [5 ed.]); M.I. Handel, 'Deception, surprise, intelligence', chapter 15 in *Masters of War* (London: Routledge, 2001 [3 ed.]); J. Ångström and J.J. Widén, *Contemporary Military Theory* (London: Routledge, 2015); B.J. Sutherland, ed., *Modern Warfare, Intelligence and Deterrence* (London: Wiley, 2011); J.A. Ravndal, 'Developing intelligence capabilities in support of UN peace operations', *NUPI Report* (Oslo: December 2009); D. Jordan et al., *Understanding Modern Warfare* (Cambridge: Cambridge University Press, 2016 [2 ed.]); J. Tama, 'Why strategic planning matters to national security', *Lawfare*; P. Porter, 'The weight of the punch: British ambition and power', *War on the Rocks* (6–7 March 2016); S. Watts, 'How the U.S. can better help militaries around the world', *Lawfare* (4 May 2016); E.J. Avery, M. Graham, and S. Park, 'Planning makes (closer to) perfect: Exploring United States' local government officials' evaluations of crisis management', *Journal of Contingences and Crisis Management* (2016); M.K. Sparrow, 'Opinion: Moving beyond Bratton', *New York Times* (8 August 2016).

12. See, e.g., as outlined in D.S. Reveron and J.L. Cook, 'From national to theater: Developing strategy', *Joint Forces Quarterly*, 70 (2013), pp. 113–20.

13. Svendsen, 'Advancing "defence-in-depth"', p. 61; A.D.M. Svendsen, 'Contemporary intelligence innovation in practice', *Defence Studies*, 15, 2 (2015), p. 113; 'The six steps in the intelligence cycle' figure in US ODNI, *U.S. National Intelligence: An Overview 2013* (Washington, DC: April 2013), p. 4; see also models and methods in R.M. Clark, *Intelligence Analysis* (Washington, DC: CQ Press, 2012 [4 ed.]); R.M. Clark and W.L. Mitchell, *Target-Centric Network Modeling* (Washington, DC: CQ Press, 2015).

14. On these, e.g., Svendsen, *The Professionalization of Intelligence Cooperation*, p. 116; Svendsen, 'Advancing "defence-in-depth"', pp. 60–61; M. Degaut, 'Spies and policymakers: Intelligence in the information age', *Intelligence and National Security* (2015); C.M. Poplin, 'Pentagon releases new procedures for intelligence collection', *Lawfare* (10 August 2016).

15. See also A.D.M. Svendsen, 'Sharpening SOF tools, their strategic use and direction', *Defence Studies*, 14, 3 (2014), pp. 284–309; Editorial, 'Special operations forces deserve "budget stability"', *Defense News* (9 May 2016); T. Joscelyn, 'Presence of French special forces in Libya sets off controversy', *Long War Journal* (22 July 2016); M. Ryan and S. Raghavan, 'U.S. special operations troops aiding Libyan forces in major battle against Islamic State', *Washington Post*; P. Lohaus, 'In Afghanistan, special operators continue to burn both ends of the candle', *Cipher Brief* (9/18 August 2016); D. Madden et al., *Toward Operational Art in Special Warfare* (Santa

Monica: Rand Corporation, 2016); V. Finan, 'Moment Western troops use a Javelin anti-tank missile launcher to take out a "Mad-Max-style" ISIS car bomb', *Daily Mail*; K. Dozier, 'U.S. special ops kill 40 ISIS operatives responsible for attacks from Paris to Egypt', *The Daily Beast* (26/28 April 2016); J. Moran, 'Assessing SOF transparency and accountability', *Remote Control Report* (4 July 2016); A. Moloney and M. Rowling, 'Gangs, crime and slums: Growing cities present new challenges for aid agencies', Reuters (17 May 2016); S. Sassen 'Three emergent migrations: An epochal change', *Conectas Human Rights* (22 July 2016); J. Braude and T. Jiang, 'Expertise in countering urban street gangs can be used to fight Jihadists', Foreign Policy Research Institute; J.E. Barnes, 'European terrorism arrests rise as Jihadist groups focus on urban attacks', *Wall Street Journal* (20 July 2016). On 'mission-creep', see Svendsen, *Understanding the Globalization of Intelligence*, p. 125; M. Townsend, 'Counter-terrorism is a relentless challenge to spot the critical intelligence', *Guardian* (27 March 2016); M. Pomerleau, 'How STRATCOM's priorities line up in an interconnected world', C4ISRNet; L. Penn-Hall, 'Russia, China: Cyber espionage', *Cipher Brief*; 'Australia seizes record cocaine haul on cruise ship, arrests three Canadians', Reuters; S. Banister, A. Adams, and R. Gerona, 'Fentanyl and other synthetic opioids sold as counterfeits in deadly new trend', *The Conversation* (16/28/29 August 2016).

16. See also Svendsen, 'Advancing "defence-in-depth"', p. 65 and p. 67; Svendsen, *The Professionalization of Intelligence Cooperation*, p. 22; on 'contextualisation' more generally, see Svendsen, *Intelligence Cooperation and the War on Terror*, p. 233, col. 2; see also challenging cases, e.g., 'Anthony Long: Officer cleared after Azelle Rodney shooting attacks IPCC', BBC (9 August 2016).

17. See, e.g., the figure published in Svendsen, 'Advancing "defence-in-depth"', p. 66.

18. J.O. Weatherall, *The Physics of Finance—Predicting the Unpredictable* (London: Short Books, 2014), p. 206.

19. Svendsen, *Understanding the Globalization of Intelligence*, p. 12 (emphasis added); cf. different 'levels of war' in J. Ångström and J.J. Widén, *Contemporary Military Theory* (London: Routledge, 2015), esp. p. 203, col. 2; Jordan et al., *Understanding Modern Warfare*, pp. 13–14.

20. Svendsen, 'Advancing "defence-in-depth"', p. 64; Svendsen, 'Contemporary intelligence innovation in practice', p. 112; see also 'A systems approach to nuclear security, non-proliferation, deterrence and disarmament', *BASIC* (August 2016).

21. Svendsen, *Understanding the Globalization of Intelligence*, pp. 99–107; A.D.M. Svendsen, 'Intelligence liaison', *Intelligencer—AFIO* (May 2015).

22. See throughout Svendsen, 'Advancing "defence-in-depth"' and Svendsen, 'Contemporary intelligence innovation in practice'; see also esp. '4.1 Getting started checklist' and '4.3 Customer checklist' as detailed in chapter 4, 'Decomposition and visualisation', of Heuer, Jr. and Pherson, *Structured Analytic Techniques for Intelligence Analysis*.

23. See also for a depiction of System of Systems Analysis (SoSA) in the U.S. military context, figure IV-2 from US Joint Chiefs of Staff, *Joint Publication J-P 3.0* (August 2011), p. IV-5. For more in-depth discussion of SoSA and its applied use with regard to intelligence, see Svendsen, 'Advancing "defence-in-depth"', from p. 58; Svendsen, 'Contemporary intelligence innovation in practice', from p. 109.

24. See also K. Sholes, 'Shrinking the tactical civilian–military divide', *War on the Rocks* (11 April 2016); see also the SATs as detailed in 'Decision support', chapter 11 of Heuer, Jr. and Pherson, *Structured Analytic Techniques for Intelligence Analysis*.

25. G. Segell, 'Book Review: International intelligence cooperation and accountability', *Political Studies Review*, 10, 3 (2012), pp. 410–11; see also the introduction to this book; similar refs in Svendsen, *Understanding the Globalization of Intelligence*, p. 54 and p. 93; equally, see the different, overlapping dimensions presented in figure 3.2—'*Geospatially Oriented Aspects of the Information Domain of the Operating Environment*' in E.V. Larson et al., *Assessing Irregular Warfare: A Framework for Intelligence Analysis* (Rand Corporation, 2008), p. 25.

26. See A.D.M. Svendsen, 'Introducing RESINT', *International Journal of Intelligence and CounterIntelligence*, 26, 4 (2013), pp. 777–94; A.D.M. Svendsen, 'Collective intelligence (COLINT)' in G. Moore, ed., *Encyclopedia of U.S. Intelligence* (New York: CRC, 2014); T.W. Malone and M.S. Bernstein, eds., *Handbook of Collective Intelligence* (Cambridge, MA: MIT Press, 2015); C. Hobbs et al., eds., *Open Source Intelligence in the Twenty-First Century* (Basingstoke, UK: Palgrave Macmillan, 2014); B. Miller, 'Evolution of intel: How valuable is OSINT?' *In Public Safety* (24 July 2015); F. Konkel, 'CIA Director: open source a "tremendous advantage"', Nextgov.com (26 July 2016); see also D. Omand et al., 'Introducing social media intelligence (SOCMINT)', *Intelligence and National Security*, 27, 6 (September 2012), pp. 801–23; M. Hamaid, 'Social media intelligence: Successes, challenges; future prospects', *JAIPIO*, 23, 3 (2015), pp. 3–21; T.E. Nissen, *#TheWeaponizationOfSocialMedia* (Copenhagen: Royal Danish Defence College, 2015); A.D.M. Svendsen, 'NATO, Libya operations and intelligence co-operation—A step forward?' *Baltic Security and Defence Review*, 13, 2 (December 2011), p. 59; 'US spy map agency charts Syrian exodus using social media', Nextgov.com (17 March 2016); T.E. Nissen, 'Twitter's role in modern warfare', BBC (21 March 2016); S. Jones, 'Social media's impact on war', *Diplomatic Courier* (28 July 2016); M. Pomerleau, 'NGA, NRO stand up joint commercial geoint activity', C4ISRNet (12 August 2016).

27. C. Clark, 'Carter details cyber, intel strikes against Daesh at NORTHCOM ceremony', *Breaking Defense* (13 May 2016); K.G. Coleman, 'Cyber intelligence—A big issue', C4ISRNet (13 June 2016); S.J. Freedberg, Jr., 'Fight against Islamic State not COIN, increasingly high tech: Carter', *Breaking Defense* (27 July 2016); M. Pomerleau, 'How are U.S. allies targeting ISIS on the cyber front?'; K. Coleman, 'The growing importance of cyber intelligence', C4ISRNet; 'Kuwait detains member of Islamic State cyber army—Newspapers', Reuters (4/9/26 August 2016).

28. On SoSE activities and further insights relating to how they connect with SoSA, Svendsen, 'Advancing "defence-in-depth"'; and Svendsen, 'Contemporary intelligence innovation in practice'.

29. See also, e.g., Svendsen, *Intelligence Cooperation and the War on Terror*, pp. 157–58; G. Tecuci, et al., *Intelligence Analysis as Discovery of Evidence, Hypotheses, and Arguments* (Cambridge: CUP, 2016).

30. Blank templates of each of the maps can be found in the appendix.

31. The slides in this section draw mainly on two conference presentations, A.D.M. Svendsen, 'Making it STARC! Proposed future ways forward for contemporary military and special operations intelligence and knowledge work', International

Symposium on Military Operational Research 2015 (Royal Holloway, University of London: July 2015); and (b) 'Advancing system of systems dynamics (SoSD) in the cyber intelligence (CYBINT) domain', *International Society of Military Sciences Conference 2015* (Helsinki: Finnish Defence University, October 2015).

32. For recent insights into the Islamic State, inter alia, A.D.M. Svendsen, 'Developing international intelligence liaison against Islamic State', *International Journal of Intelligence and CounterIntelligence*, 29, 2 (2016), pp. 260–77; J. Stern and J.M. Berger, *ISIS* (London: Collins, 2016); J. Burke, *The New Threat from Islamic Militancy* (London: Vintage, 2016); L. Robinson, 'ISIS vs special ops: One half of a good strategy', *Foreign Affairs* (7 December 2015); O. Dorell, 'Intelligence officials: ISIL determined to strike U.S. this year', *USA Today* (9 February 2016); see also earlier discussion of the cyber domain in chapter 2.

33. See also, e.g., N. Ashdown, 'Policy gaming the risk of escalation in the Syrian conflict', IHS Jane's 360 (5 February 2016); 'Gaming and public policy: Q&A with David Shlapak', Rand Corporation (11 August 2016); and chapters in W.J. Lahneman and R. Arcos, eds., *The Art of Intelligence* (New York: Rowman & Littlefield, 2014).

34. See also refs to these areas in Svendsen, 'Advancing "defence-in-depth"', p. 67; E. Selinger, 'Why does our privacy really matter?' *Christian Science Monitor* (22 April 2016); J.G. Carter et al., 'Law enforcement fusion centers', *Journal of Police and Criminal Psychology* (May 2016); for the added value of enterprise thinking, see, e.g., A.D.M. Svendsen with M. von Rosing, H. von Scheel, and A-W. Scheer et al., 'Business process trends' in *The Complete Business Process Handbook—Volume 1* (Burlington, MA: Morgan Kaufmann/Elsevier, 2014), from p. 187; N. Hare and P. Coghill, 'The future of the intelligence analysis task', *Intelligence and National Security* (January 2016); 'Looking to enterprise for an intel boost', C4ISRNet (9 May 2014); A. Corrin, 'Enterprise IT: Advanced tech top intel budget goals', C4ISRNet (9 February 2016); 'CIA names intelligence community IT pro as CIO', *Wall Street Journal* (18 March 2016); Svendsen, 'Intelligence, surveillance and reconnaissance (ISR)'; A. Corrin, 'Intel community looks to life after TPED', C4ISRNet (16 April 2015); 'Pentagon awards HP Enterprise $443 million technology contract', Reuters (21 April 2016); A. Corrin, 'Integrating C4ISR into DoD', C4ISRNet (25 April 2016); F. Konkel, 'The future of intelligence sharing is coming together in the Syrian war', *Defense One*; S. Losey, 'JTACs using live video feeds to target ISIS', *Air Force Times* (28 April 2016); 'No more ransom: Law enforcement and IT security companies join forces to fight ransomware', *Business Wire* (25 July 2016); A. Boyd, '4 major changes coming to DoD intel policy'; 'How industry can help DoD with new intel policy', C4ISRNet; 'Open architecture bringing benefits to Air Force DCGS', *Air Force Link*; M. Peck, 'Air Force wants more TID-BIT', C4ISRNet (1/25/29 August 2016); see also related discussion and sources above in chapter 2.

35. See, e.g., how an 'operational picture' is built up as illustrated in '*Figure 5.5: Tools to create shared "situational awareness"*' in W.L. Perry et al., *Predictive Policing* (Santa Monica, CA: Rand Corporation, 2013), p. 130; N. Quarmby, 'Futures work in strategic criminal intelligence', conference paper (Canberra, Australia: 2003); A. Swanson, 'Wonkblog: The eerie math that could predict terrorist attacks',

Washington Post (1 March 2016); D.G. Perkins, 'Big picture, not details, key when eyeing future', *Army Magazine* (12 April 2016).

36. See as demonstrated in A.D.M. Svendsen, 'Discovering "unknown-unknowns" & beyond', conference paper, *33rd International Symposium on Military Operational Research Conference* (Royal Holloway, London, 2016); see also as demonstrated in '*Figure 7.6: Sherman Kent chart, converting qualitative judgments in quantitative terms (and vice versa)*' in J. Clauser and J. Goldman (rev. ed.), *An Introduction to Intelligence Research and Analysis* (Lanham, MD: Scarecrow Press, 2008), p. 89.

37. For similar 'indicator-based' approaches, 'Strategic early warning for criminal intelligence: Theoretical framework and sentinel methodology', *Criminal Intelligence Service Canada* (Ottawa, ON: CISC, 2007); M.D. Phillips, 'Time series applications to intelligence analysis', *Intelligence and National Security*, 31, 5 (2016), pp. 729–45; see also 'Assessing the risk of violent extremists', *Research Summary*, 14, 5 (September 2009); D.E. Pressman, 'Risk assessment decisions for violent political extremism', *User Report 2009-02* (Ottawa: Public Safety Canada, 2009); M. Lewontin, 'Could online counter-narratives help curb ISIS's influence?' *Christian Science Monitor* (25 February 2016); S.R. Corman, 'The narrative rationality of violent extremism', *Social Science Quarterly*, 97 (2016), pp. 9–18; A. Päll, 'Ministers risk missing the point on radicalisation', EurActiv.com (29 February 2016); J. Klausen, T. Morrill, and R. Libretti, 'The terrorist age-crime curve', *Social Science Quarterly*, 97 (2016), pp. 19–32; see also the SATs outlined throughout chapter 6, 'Scenarios and indicators' in Heuer, Jr. and Pherson, *Structured Analytic Techniques for Intelligence Analysis*.

38. For the utility of mainstream business/management insights with regard to intelligence contexts, see Svendsen, *The Professionalization of Intelligence Cooperation*, p. 7, p. 21, p. 71.

39. See also as elaborated in A.D.M. Svendsen, 'Strategic futures and intelligence', (draft article); A.D.M. Svendsen, 'International intelligence liaison: A primer', *Romanian Journal of Intelligence Studies* (2016); see also 'CLTC Scenarios', Center for Long-Term Cybersecurity (University of California, Berkeley, April 2016); S. Malo, 'Governments should study worst-case global warming scenarios, former UN official says', Reuters; P. Tucker, 'America's new special operations commander wants to predict the future', *Defense One* (4/25 May 2016).

40. See as characterised throughout Svendsen, *Understanding the Globalization of Intelligence*; Svendsen, *The Professionalization of Intelligence Cooperation*; Svendsen, *Intelligence Cooperation and the War on Terror*; A.D.M. Svendsen, 'An intelligence-engineering framework for defence engagement considerations', paper presented at the *Human Geography in Defence Engagement: 9th Annual International Spatial Socio-Cultural Knowledge Workshop* (Shrivenham: UK Defence Academy & Cranfield University, May 2016); Svendsen, 'Discovering "unknown-unknowns" & beyond'; R.R. Greene Sands, *Assessing Special Operations Forces Language, Region, and Culture Needs* (MacDill AFB, FL: Joint Special Operations University Press, August 2016); A. Zwitter, *Humanitarian Intelligence* (New York: Rowman & Littlefield, 2016); A. Gharib, 'The fog of unknowing', *Republic*; S. Aftergood, 'Knowing the enemy: DoD identity activities', *FAS Secrecy News* (23 August 2016); see also as discussed further in chapter 4.

41. On this thinking, see Svendsen, *Understanding the Globalization of Intelligence*, esp. p. 78, p. 124, p. 147; Svendsen, *The Professionalization of Intelligence Cooperation*, esp. pp. 45–46, p. 69, p. 123, p. 160.

42. Svendsen, 'Advancing "defence-in-depth"', p. 66; B. Rosenberg and J. Edwards, 'How SOSE&I is synchronizing Army IT efforts', C4ISRNet (28 March 2016); K. Mills, 'How to survive the surveillance video data flood', *Government Computer News* (15 April 2016); T. Ripley, 'British Army watchkeeper UAV downed by computer glitch', IHS Jane's 360 (16 August 2016); F.P.B. Osinga, *Science, Strategy and War* (London: Routledge, 2007); J.A. Olsen, ed., *Airpower Reborn* (Annapolis, MD: NIP, 2015).

43. Svendsen, 'Contemporary intelligence innovation in practice', pp. 112–13; K. Lim, 'Big data and strategic intelligence', *Intelligence and National Security* (2015); see other citations to 'big data' throughout this study, as well as refs to its implications and '4Vs' considerations, as detailed in chapter 1; see also A. Burdick et al., *Digital_Humanities* (London: MIT Press, 2012).

44. Svendsen, 'Intelligence, surveillance and reconnaissance (ISR)'; see also the paradoxes as highlighted in Svendsen, 'Developing international intelligence liaison against Islamic State', esp. p. 265, p. 269; J. Judson, 'US Army special operations has big appetite for ISR', *Defense News* (9 May 2016); K. Lunney, 'As wars demand intel, Air Force boosts drone pilot bonuses', *Defense One* (12 August 2016).

45. Svendsen, 'Collective intelligence (COLINT)' and as introduced above; see also the introduction.

46. See also as detailed in the introduction; A.D.M. Svendsen, 'Buffeted not busted: The UKUSA "Five Eyes" after Snowden', *e-IR.info* (8 January 2014); Svendsen, 'Intelligence liaison', *Intelligencer*; P.F. Walsh and S. Miller, 'Rethinking "Five Eyes" security intelligence collection policies and practice post Snowden'; R.G. Patman and L. Southgate, 'National security and surveillance: The public impact of the GCSB amendment bill and the Snowden revelations in New Zealand', *Intelligence and National Security* (2015); A. Young, 'Keeping the balance for security agencies'; I. Davison, 'Labour spells out spying bottom lines', *NZ Herald*; I. MacLeod, 'Spying on Canadian phone calls and emails by Canadian SIGINT agency has risen dramatically', *Ottawa Citizen* (20/22/24 August 2016).

47. See chapter 2; A.D.M. Svendsen, '"Smart law" for intelligence!' *Tech and Law Center* (University of Milan, Italy: June 2015); O. Bowcott, 'Jean Charles de Menezes: Police officers should not be prosecuted, says ECHR', *Guardian* (30 March 2016); Svendsen, 'Re-fashioning risk', p. 314; 'Drone killings: Legal case "needs clarifying"', BBC; A. Ross and O. Bowcott, 'UK drone strikes "could leave all those involved facing murder charges"', *Guardian* (10 May 2016).

48. On event and development curve concepts, Svendsen, *Understanding the Globalization of Intelligence*, p. 78, p. 124, p. 147; Svendsen, *The Professionalization of Intelligence Cooperation*, p. 123, p. 160; Svendsen, *Intelligence Cooperation and the War on Terror*, p. 40, p. 58; B. Wittes and D.L. Byman, 'Flowchart: How the government handles a terrorist threat', Brookings Institution (Washington, DC: 2013); T. Watkins, 'US releases redacted drone strike "playbook"', *AFP/Military Times*

(7 August 2016); S. Miglani, 'U.S. says 300 Islamic State fighters killed in Afghan operation', Reuters; C. Reuter, 'Retreat and delusion: Is the Islamic State finally collapsing?' *Spiegel Online*, L.C. Baldor, 'US: 45,000 Islamic State fighters taken off battlefields', Associated Press; J. Steele, '*LA Times*: U.S. intel sees ISIS as weakened after defeats', *San Diego Union Tribune*; M. Weiss, 'Leaked ISIS documents show internal chaos', *The Daily Beast*; 'Key Islamic State leader killed in apparent U.S. strike in Syria', Reuters (10/11/29/30/31 August 2016).

Chapter Four

Advancing an IE-Based Framework for Risk

This chapter presents an annotated, step-by-step walk-through of a currently evolving IE-based framework for risk. Building on the IE-related concepts and tools introduced in chapter 3, this chapter further demonstrates (1) how different IE components are continuing to develop, (2) how they can be better harnessed, and (3) how they can be brought together in, first, overarching risk analysis/assessment (estimate) work, and second, risk management and resilience enterprises that extend into the future.[1] A series of 'bite-size' framework process steps are presented throughout, with illustrative figures to further explain the process and how it should work.

STEP 1: FOCUS SELECTION—
TARGETING AND PRIORITISATION

Step 1 concentrates on the important starting dimension of *focus* (see figure 4.1). Notably, this step concerns helping to answer core beginning questions such as *What should be examined (further)?* and *How should it be ranked or categorised?*[2]

The work in this step is also multi-scaler in that it can focus on, inter alia, *anything* from a big 'theme', such as *cyber* or *globalisation*, down to a particular 'issue'. So, rather than having a broad scope, work in this step can instead focus more precisely on more specific entities, such as a particular problem that might need various degrees of trouble-shooting towards its solving.

Essentially, the possibility exists that *whatever* is focused on can then be examined in-depth, together with offering the potential that the subject of focus

(1) Choose focus:
Theme(s)/
Issue(s)/
Problem(s)/
Hazard(s)/
Risk(s)/
Threat(s)

Step 1

- Step 1 concerns **'targeting' + 'prioritisation'**

- Provides answer to question - e.g.: **'What to focus on?'** during intelligence enterprises/activities (missions, jobs, operations), however scaled.

- In this example, a particular 'risk' = selected.

Figure 4.1. STEP 1: Focus
Courtesy of the Author

can be subsequently tracked and traced, relating to going both forwards and backwards through the overall process and along its progression (see below). This effort is framed, for instance, in terms of choosing specific, determined locations (e.g., in country *X*) and then travelling over different selected time-frames or timelines (e.g., short-term, mid-term, to long-term). In keeping with current demands, the qualities of agility, adaptability, and flexibility all remain. Refined and consistent targeting in a prioritising manner is necessary to maintain adequate perspective and at least a degree of analytic continuity.[3] Once we have our focus, we move on to step 2.

STEP 2—WHICH SYSTEM OF SYSTEMS DYNAMICS (SOSD)?

Step 2 focuses on which SoSD units we should select for further examination during the overall IE process (see figure 4.2). This is for the purposes of, first, analysis (SoSA), and then which areas should be focused upon for subsequent engineering (SoSE). As a rough guide, (1) STEEP(L)—social, technological, economic, environmental, political, and legal or legislative units should be drawn upon as they are commonly used in commercial and business intelligence–related contexts; (2) PESTLE—political, economic, social, technological, legal or legislative, and environmental units should be drawn upon in contexts related to those navigated by EUROPOL, such as the tackling of cyber and transnational and organised crime; (3) PME-SII—political, military, economic, social, informational or intelligence, and infrastructural units should be harnessed in relation to contexts associated with the North Atlantic Treaty Organisation (NATO), such as crisis management and other activities in operational spaces and battlespaces; (4) DIME—diplomatic, informational, military, and economic units; and (5) HSCB—human, social, cultural, and behavioural dimensions—should be drawn upon in contexts similar to those negotiated by entities such as the U.S. Military both in war zones and in relation to humanitarian and disaster-relief operations.[4] Once we have identified and selected the requisite SoSD units of analysis and engineering—ideally most appropriately and justifiably attuned to the task at hand or to the circumstances and contexts encountered (post facto, after the event) or expected to be experienced (a priori or more pre-emptively, before developments so that, e.g., prevention is stressed)—it is time to move on to step 3.

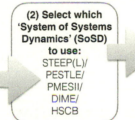

Step 2

- Provides guide as to: **'What "units of analysis" or systems should be drawn upon?'**

- For example, PMESII: Political, Military, Economic, Social, Infrastructural, Informational/Intelligence, etc.

- Above form the units of analysis or systems as **widely + conventionally used** in, e.g. NATO.

Figure 4.2. STEP 2: System of Systems Dynamics
Courtesy of the Author

Step 3

- **Each of the units of analysis or systems** drawn on + ref. in prev. slide - e.g. social +/or political - can be **further broken-down** into their **different variables or attributes** during analysis.

(3) Each 'system' in SoSD has following variables/attributes:
(i) *internal influences/factors*;
(ii) *rationale*;
(iii) *types & forms*;
(iv) *conditions & terms*;
(v) *trends (inc. SWOT)*;
(vi) *functions*;
(vii) *external influences/factors*;
+
(viii)
effects & outcomes

Figure 4.3.   STEP 3: System attributes or variables
Courtesy of the Author

STEP 3—GOING DEEPER INTO SYSTEM
ATTRIBUTES AND VARIABLES

Step 3 takes each SoSD unit of analysis and engineering and then breaks each of those systems down further into its constitutive system(-atic/-ic) attributes, or variables. In the case of the IE framework advanced here, there are eight system(-atic/-ic) attributes (see figure 4.3 and chapter 3).[5] Once we have ascertained each of these system(-atic/-ic) attributes (or have done so as far as possible), we can then further parse them into different levels, as step 4 details.

STEP 4—EXTENDING FURTHER INTO
DIFFERENT LEVEL CONSIDERATIONS

In this step, the above system(-atic/-ic) attributes, or variables, are broken down into eight different levels relating to experience (see figure 4.4). These different levels, in turn, each then communicate other considerations, which we must also

Step 4

- **Every system variable or attribute** ref. on prev. slide & worked on in prev. framework/process step - e.g. 'rationale' **>>> evaluated further**.

- They each have **8 different, informing 'levels' of experience**, which >>> also drawn on during analysis.

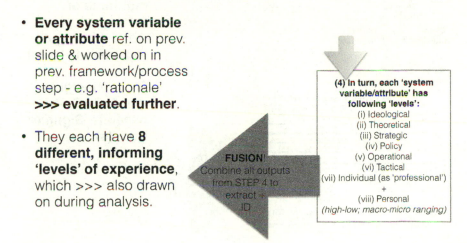

FUSION! Combine all outputs from STEP 4 to extract + ID

(4) In turn, each 'system variable/attribute' has following 'levels':
(i) Ideological
(ii) Theoretical
(iii) Strategic
(iv) Policy
(v) Operational
(vi) Tactical
(vii) Individual (as 'professional')
+
(viii) Personal
(high-low; macro-micro ranging)

Figure 4.4. STEP 4: Levels
Courtesy of the Author

take into account. By doing this work, a comprehensive and holistic approach towards the challenges confronted is better advanced so that no particular area is neglected or overlooked—or indeed, equally, is over-emphasised—in, for example, an overly reductionist manner or at the expense of other areas that might also be involved in the overall mix. Effective balancing remains key.[6]

STEP 5—BRINGING EVERYTHING ALL TOGETHER!

In step 5 we rationalise all of the factors harvested from the work undertaken during the course of steps 1–4. This is so that the output from those steps can be communicated both as and into distilled insights relevant to the A + B + C factors (see figure 4.5). As shown in chapter 3, we can accomplish this work most expeditiously and transparently using the different tabulation/grid-mapping tools and matrices (see figures 3.4–3.9; see also the blank templates provided in the appendix). Through the use of these schematics, all workings and insights can be, firstly, structured (at least to some extent) through being clearly laid out; and, secondly, readily displayed—again, in a highly transparent manner—for communication, dissemination, future follow-up, re-checking, forwards and backwards traceability, accountability and oversight, further annotation, subsequent sharing, and so forth.[7]

Step 5

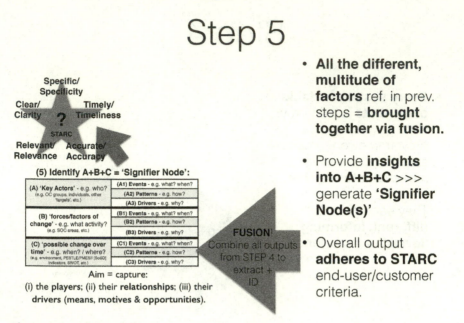

- **All the different, multitude of factors** ref. in prev. steps = **brought together via fusion.**

- Provide **insights into A+B+C** >>> generate **'Signifier Node(s)'**

- Overall output **adheres to STARC** end-user/customer criteria.

Figure 4.5. STEP 5: Fusion
Courtesy of the Author

We obtain further A insights, relating to 'Key Actors', by conducting 'Network Analytic' work and using associated tools and platforms—for instance, through embarking on 'Analysis Related to Persons, Other Entities, and Relationships of Interest'. Our B inputs, regarding 'Forces/Factors of Change', we obtain by using 'Narrative Tools'; namely, drawing on 'Records and Notes on Entities and Events of Interest'. Meanwhile our C insights, relating to 'Possible Change over Time', we ascertain by engaging in 'Spatiotemporal Analytics' work, notably harnessing the tools and platforms that present 'Analysis Related to Where and When Crime [(as highlighted in this example)] Might Occur'.[8]

Probing deeper, we find that hand-in-glove with the above work are suitably complementary lead-ins and overlaps to further-ranging methodologies, such as 'Structured Brainstorming', 'Cross-Impact Matrix', and 'Quadrant Crunching' structured analytic technique (SAT) approaches—to cite three most readily apparent examples from the several that currently exist. We find these SATs elaborated upon further within the offerings from an increasingly established professional body of intelligence analysis education and training titled Structured Analytic Techniques for Intelligence Analysis, which is employed internationally on a widespread basis. SATs allow us to harness many diverse data inputs using both qualitative and quantitative approaches.[9]

Armed with the A + B + C factors—again, through applying adequate due diligence and through justifiable, explicit labelling or highlighting on the maps—then the 'signifier nodes' emerge more clearly. These give at least *operational pictures* and degrees of *situational awareness*, adhering to the intelligence customer or end-user requirements of STARC (see chapter 3).

The A + B + C insights essentially cluster around and capture three key elements: (1) the players, (2) their relationships, and (3) their drivers (means, motives, and opportunities).[10] Ultimately, the signifier nodes are useful for helping make *Where next?* decisions and for offering strategic early warning (SEW) potential—for example, when used to provide inputs to help develop, structure, and inform wider and further-ranging strategic futures–related scenarios and similar horizon-scanning to foresight efforts.[11]

AN OVERVIEW OF THE WHOLE PROCESS

Figure 4.6 presents a summary of the entire process presented in this chapter. By following such a constructed evaluative process as has been presented,

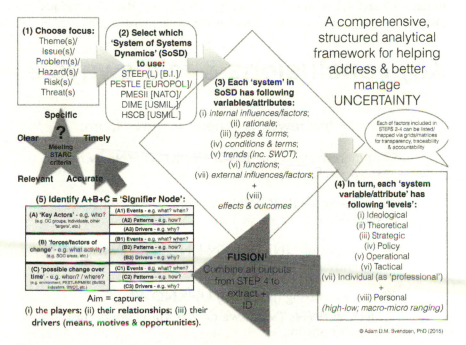

Figure 4.6. Overview/Summary
Courtesy of the Author

a more comprehensive, structured analytical framework for helping address and better manage uncertainty over different geographies and timescales is proposed. Furthermore, we can likewise advance an IE-based framework for risk, relating to both its analysis and subsequent management.

There is considerable in-built flexibility and adaptability. Followed linearly (as presented), the overall process can be repeated any number of times depending on particular producer and end-user needs or requirements, including taking into account observed and even wrought changes from previous efforts, inputs from 'new challenges', and so forth. By appropriately adjusting the different factors or aspects involved in each of the steps, reasonable adaption is also possible, such as through the carefully controlled recalibration of those dimensions as we reconfigure the overall process for its next iteration or rendering. This includes being careful not to adjust too many factors or variables all at once or at any one time so that perspective is lost rather than gained. A sustained degree of control is required to maintain adequate overall command.

CONCLUSIONS

Figures 4.7 and 4.8 summarise the utility of adopting the IE-associated approaches introduced in chapter 3 and put into demonstrable action in this

Key **conclusions** & **takeaways** #1

- Tools + frameworks = help us move from:

  ➡ (i) merely exploiting **KNOWN-KNOWNs** ('what we know we know') >>>

  ➡ (ii) exploring **KNOWN-UNKNOWNs** ('what we know we do not know') >>>

  ➡ (iii) exposing **UNKNOWN-KNOWNs** ('what we do not know we know') +

  ➡ (iv) discovering (potential) **UNKNOWN-UNKNOWNs** ('what we do not know we do not know') domains.

Figure 4.7.   Key Insights #1
Courtesy of the Author

chapter. Most immediately, these approaches allow us to generate an improved understanding of the challenges we currently confront, regardless of whether we conceptualise these challenges as full-spectrum issues, problems, hazards, risks, or threats. Without the adoption of this at least semi-structured, analytical approach, ignorance and knowledge-atrophy are more likely to prevail. This includes relating to any 'unknowns'.[12]

The overall IE-related process proposed here should be embarked upon repeatedly, on each occasion of its progression altering the different aspects or factors that feature in the different steps accordingly. This adjustment is undertaken through the adequately controlled reconfiguration and recalibration of each factor to maintain focus and perspective, which then extends to an overall command regarding what is unfolding. In this way, a constantly looping, suitably evolving iterative process is represented, and we are thus able to account for, even demonstrate, dynamic changes and adaptions/adaptations to other updates, while gaining insight into areas such as when and where those attributes might occur. We benefit from an in-depth approach to improved contextualisation undertaken in a more simplified and step-by-step manner. The adoption of these logical and more manageable approaches helps guide.[13]

In the highly complex environments encountered and characterised earlier, we cannot allow information vacuums or other areas of paucity to succeed.

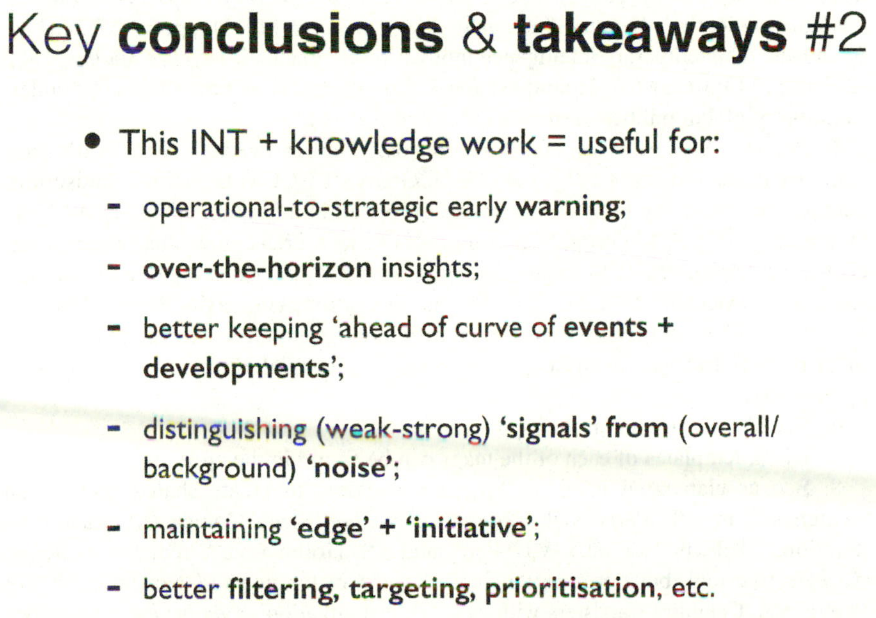

Key conclusions & takeaways #2

- This INT + knowledge work = useful for:

  - operational-to-strategic early **warning**;

  - **over-the-horizon** insights;

  - better keeping 'ahead of curve of **events + developments**';

  - distinguishing (weak-strong) **'signals' from** (overall/ background) **'noise'**;

  - maintaining **'edge' + 'initiative'**;

  - better **filtering, targeting, prioritisation**, etc.

Figure 4.8. Key Insights #2
Courtesy of the Author

Otherwise, we can readily anticipate detrimental outcomes for a wide range of participants and stakeholders both now and in the future. In the concluding chapter of this book, offered for further consideration is a potential guide to the future, or at least a series of insights into those areas we must be *sensitive of* and *aware of* in the future.

NOTES

1. See also insights in J-M. Normandin and M-C. Therrien, 'Resilience factors reconciled with complexity: The dynamics of order and disorder', *Journal of Contingencies and Crisis Management* (2016); C. Fjäder, 'The nation-state, national security and resilience in the age of globalisation', *Resilience*, 2, 2 (2014), pp. 114–29.

2. See also E. Groll, 'U.S. spy chiefs think the world is pretty much going to hell', *Foreign Policy*; A. Capaccio, 'Carter cites do-it-all pressure on $583 billion defense plan', Bloomberg; S.D. Krasner and A. Zegart, 'A clear-eyed focus on our interests: A guide for the next president', *War on the Rocks* (9/11 February 2016).

3. See A.D.M. Svendsen, *Understanding the Globalization of Intelligence* (Basingstoke, UK: Palgrave Macmillan, 2012), esp. p. 53, p. 71, p. 78, p. 89, p. 129, pp. 131–32; A.D.M. Svendsen, *The Professionalization of Intelligence Cooperation* (Basingstoke, UK: Palgrave Macmillan, 2012), esp. p. 147, p. 152, p. 157; A.D.M. Svendsen, *Intelligence Cooperation and the War on Terror* (London: Routledge, 2010), esp. p. 14, p. 59, p. 69, p. 93, p. 98, pp. 157–58; A.D.M. Svendsen, 'Advancing "defence-in-depth"', *Defense & Security Analysis*, 31, 1 (2015), pp. 66–67; A.D.M. Svendsen, 'Contemporary intelligence innovation in practice', *Defence Studies*, 15, 2 (2015), p. 113; see also C. Holmqvist and T. Lundborg, 'How time shapes our understanding of global politics', *e-ir.info* (16 August 2016).

4. See also, e.g., K. Pavgi and P. Kouretsos, 'The US needs to whip its disaster-response plans into shape', *Defense One*; J. Grady, 'EUCOM Breedlove: Indiscriminate Russian bombing in Syria worsening European immigration crisis', *USNI News* (1 March 2016); G. Moulson, 'German gov't oks new crisis guidelines, rejects criticism', Associated Press (24 August 2016); R. Post and J.D. Peterson, *Unconventional Economics* (MacDill AFB, FL: Joint Special Operations University Press, 2016).

5. For further details of what the eight different system attributes/variables consist of at their fullest, see Svendsen, *Understanding the Globalization of Intelligence*, pp. 99–107.

6. See also discussion in *ibid.*, pp. 106–7.

7. Blank templates of each of the maps can be found in the appendix.

8. See as elaborated upon in 'Figure 5.5: Tools to create shared "situational awareness"' in W.L. Perry et al., *Predictive Policing* (Santa Monica, CA: Rand Corporation, 2013), p. 130; also W.L. Perry and J.S. Hollywood, 'Predictive policing: An effective tool, but not a crystal ball', Rand Corporation (15 November 2013); 'KeyLines: Catching fraudsters with network visualization', *Cambridge Intelligence* (2016).

9. See the SATs '5.1 Structured brainstorming', '5.5 Cross-impact matrix', and '5.7 Quadrant crunching' as explained further in chapter 5 of R.J. Heuer, Jr. and R.H. Pherson, *Structured Analytic Techniques for Intelligence Analysis* (Washington, DC: CQ Press, 2014 [2 ed.]); S. Coulthart, 'Why do analysts use structured analytic techniques?' *Intelligence and National Security* (March 2016).

10. See also, e.g., N. Yaraghi, 'To mitigate medical hacks, identify incentives for hackers', Brookings Institution; B. Garrett-Glaser, 'Indicators of political instability'; J. Goldstone, 'How valuable are the indicators?'; J.J. Messner, 'Measuring levels of fragility', *Cipher Brief* (16/18 August 2016); see related discussion in Svendsen, 'Contemporary intelligence innovation in practice', p. 110.

11. For further SAT links, e.g., see as included in chapter 6, 'Scenarios and indicators', and chapter 11, 'Decision support', and esp. '11.7 Complexity manager' of Heuer, Jr. and Pherson, *Structured Analytic Techniques for Intelligence Analysis*; J.S. Lockwood, *The Lockwood Analytical Method for Prediction* (London: Bloomsbury, 2013), esp. pp. 3–22.

12. See also other intelligence analysis related books, which similarly reinforce the importance of adopting 'structured-analytic' approaches and techniques in relation to differing intelligence, security and defence enterprises, e.g., R.M. Clark and W.L. Mitchell, *Target-Centric Network Modeling* (Washington, DC: CQ Press, 2015); Heuer, Jr. and Pherson, *Structured Analytic Techniques for Intelligence Analysis*; S.M. Beebe and R.H. Pherson, *Cases in Intelligence Analysis* (Washington, DC: CQ Press, 2012); A.D.M. Svendsen, 'Discovering "Unknown-unknowns" & beyond', *33rd International Symposium on Military Operational Research* (Royal Holloway, London, 2016); see also the concerns raised in W. Pincus, 'Stirring up his audience', *Cipher Brief* (9 August 2016).

13. See also L. Fisher, *The Perfect Swarm* (New York: Basic, 2009); J. Andrews, *The World in Conflict* (London: Economist/Profile, 2015); G. Priest, *Logic* (Oxford: Oxford University Press, 2000).

Part III

BRINGING IT ALL TOGETHER

Chapter Five

Conclusions and Cautions

IE is highly complex, particularly when approached and then evaluated on most comprehensive or holistic bases. However, despite its apparent overall complexity, IE readily responds to being broken down into more manageable bite-sized, constitutive aspects and dimensions. These can then be articulated further when presented as a series of steps within a structured, analytical framework for both (1) risk analysis and (2) subsequent risk management. This work is beneficial for fostering greater understanding and knowledge relating to pressing areas such as uncertainty, experienced both contemporaneously and that we can anticipate in the future. Resilience is similarly improved by further adopting these approaches.[1]

FROM SHOCKS TO LEARNING EXPERIENCES

The purpose of this chapter is to draw out this book's findings as well as to sound some cautionary notes in relation to IE, which are relevant both now and for the future. This chapter begins with a re-examination of what IE is before outlining—perhaps with more critical significance—what IE is *not*. A series of cautions relating to IE then follow, after which some answers are posed to the question *Where next for IE?* This overview allows for a further delineation of the IE landscape, which is useful for those who wish to understand and harness IE most fully and adroitly.

WHAT IE IS

Starting with the definition of IE offered in chapter 1, that definition intends to be as comprehensive as possible. It helps form the basis for better conceptualising IE as a distinct entity by describing how IE (1) fits—via its location or orientation; (2) works—via exploring its functions; and (3) does *not* succeed—by interrogating its operational parameters and limitations—in overall intelligence-related contexts. This focus includes communicating IE value and why IE deserves further examination as well as how it can constantly be subject to various associated processes, such as its continued optimisation, extension, and advancement.[2] Careful management of IE remains key as we proceed with caution.

There are a few normative insights. These emphasise how IE *should* work, both ideally and most aspirationally. The norms and values associated with a more constructivist approach to IE assist here.[3] Again, borrowing similar approaches and effectively building on the foundations of earlier findings,

> the theory-development process samples from a diverse range of what can be termed most fittingly as '*empirical and interpretive extrapolations*'. This allows both the 'scientific' and 'artistic' capture of intelligence-related phenomena. In the process, this also appropriately reflects the nature of intelligence itself, as well as helping to dilute any overly-positivist rendering.[4]

Rigorous definition of IE, such as in chapter 1, appropriately includes many different aspects. The sheer array of pluralistic qualities IE boasts suitably reflects its widespread scope of activities when its nature is taken most generally. For some analysts, the definition might be too broad. However, there is always the risk of being overly exclusionary—and to a detrimental extent—when incredibly dynamic, intelligence-related phenomena are involved. This is due to their frequent tendency to range far and wide, often eluding quick, easy, and overly narrow or brief characterisation.[5] Nor should we forget that situations reflective of 'complex co-existence plurality' may be present.[6]

BETTER ELICITING THE ENGINEERING RELATIONSHIP

Throughout this book, the relationship of engineering's several varying dimensions with respect to different aspects of intelligence becomes increasingly clear—albeit at times these proximities might come across somewhat more roughly.

What emerges most emphatically, however, is that IE has an increasing centrality. Intelligence, and by close association IE, is performing a greater role in today's world. No longer do intelligence phenomena merely *support* other functions; for better or worse, they simultaneously provide enhanced directing, even leading, pathways forward. Inter alia, this is for the negotiation of highly complicated situations, such as, again, those environments where conditions of 'complex co-existence plurality' prevail.[7]

Ultimately, it is perhaps more straightforward, and it may serve in many ways as a better reference point, to examine what IE is *not*—and, equally, what IE *should not* consist of—rather than what it is. This task forms the focus of the next section in order to continue to provide an improved delineation of IE.

WHAT IE IS NOT

By focusing on what is more 'outside' the scope of IE, we might better mitigate any potential analytical distractions or obstacles. Put another way, adopting this approach we gain an improved extraction of weak-to-strong signals relating to IE, obtained from overall conditions of persistent background noise. It is most important to highlight here that IE *is not the same as* the 'engineering *of* intelligence', with all the unhelpful connotations and implications that suggests. This has resulted in much controversy. A range of negative examples of the 'engineering of intelligence'—or perhaps what can be termed more appropriately the 'manipulation, misapplication, and misuse of intelligence'—can be readily cited. So-called dodgy dossiers and even leaks (whether officially sanctioned or not) figure significantly.[8]

Several such cases have generated dramatic headlines over the last few decades and have been subject to much—and often continuing—intense debate. This was notably seen, for instance (1) in the prominent case of the run up to the 2003 Iraq war, and (2) with regard to the many claims, even accusations, relating to the closely overlapping, so-called politicisation of intelligence, including a—at least contended—relevance to more recent intelligence assessments relating to the Islamic State (IS/ISIS/ISIL/Da'esh) in Iraq and Syria and elsewhere.[9]

NEGATIVE EFFECTS AND OUTCOMES

There are further concerns. Perhaps more worryingly, the above examples do not merely reflect conditions of 'naïve optimism' as pertaining to intelligence and how it should best be handled and used most adroitly. This is because those episodes have also been open to—at least some degree of—'wilful cynicism', that is detectable in broader manifestations.[10] As concluded in 2012,

intelligence is well known to often be an imperfect 'science' and 'art'. Verification is difficult. Intelligence frequently results in several differences of interpretation . . . . Often, this is a healthy sign and should not be dismissed. Although, likewise, there will always be people who will try to shape intelligence—as well as its analyses—to better 'fit' their own preconceived agendas.[11]

Indeed, arguably, the differences should go so far as to be instead more celebrated. Thereby, and as should always be welcome with regard to most effective intelligence enterprises, areas of further stimulation are better enabled and empowered—albeit if only in a theoretical or intellectual respect. Suitably structured, and drawing on 'scientific' approaches so that the variables in play are subject to appropriately placed degrees of command and control—such as being effectively bounded and managed—points of difference include 'thinking outside of the box', focussing on 'the other' (and 'alternatives' or 'contingencies'), and embracing potential 'redundancies'. This work involves the encompassing of 'competitive' and 'alternative analysis' methods employed, for example, during the course of intelligence analysis processes and Red/A+B Teaming exercises.[12]

IE CAUTIONS

Many of the cautions relating to IE tend to coalesce or cohere around what might be termed the 'psychology of intelligence'. These concerns likewise extend beyond the mere handling of intelligence to include the analysis of intelligence as well as more engineering-associated realms.[13] As written at much length elsewhere, the key is to *actively avoid* unfortunate situations (or 'misfortunes') and other mitigable risky conditions, such as occasions of the oft-referenced 'groupthink'.[14]

Indeed, as other analysts have asked, 'How do presidents and their advisors make war and peace decisions on military intervention, escalation, de-escalation, and termination of conflicts? How do groups make decisions? Why do they often make suboptimal decisions or appear to be frozen in inaction?' The 'groupthink' concept of group dynamics offers an explanation. Essentially, when that path is present, for example, in a presidential system akin to that in the United States, 'cohesive policymaking groups, such as advisors to the president, often make suboptimal decisions due to their desire for uniformity over dissent'. This can be while the decision- to policy-makers simultaneously ignore 'important limitations of chosen policies, overestimating the odds for success and failing to consider other relevant policy options or possibilities'.[15] In effect, essential IE-related benchmarking becomes overlooked, even more actively overridden.[16]

NEGOTIATING 'GROUPTHINK' TO 'POLYTHINK'

When embarking on IE, another aim focusses on the most expeditious way of addressing so-called and more emergent polythink hang-ups. Most ideally, mitigations to a range of negative dimensions must also continue to feature substantially. Particularly this is where the pioneers of the polythink concept have summarised and defined it as

> a group decision-making dynamic whereby different members in a decision-making unit espouse a plurality of opinions and offer divergent policy prescriptions, which can result in intragroup conflict, a disjointed decision-making process, and decision paralysis as each group member pushes for his or her preferred policy action.[17]

Alex Mintz and Carly Wayne continue, 'This phenomenon is no less problematic or common than Groupthink and explains how otherwise smart, experienced decision-makers can engage in flawed decision-making processes that deeply affect the security and welfare of a country'. In fact, as they maintain,

> by shining a light on Polythink's symptoms and consequences, and on the factors that lead to Polythink, we seek to offer actionable policy prescriptions for elite decision-makers to offset the negative attributes of this phenomenon and engage in more optimal policymaking processes. Furthermore, we explain how leaders and other decision-makers (e.g., in business) can transform Destructive Polythink into Productive Polythink, illuminating the potential ways in which this group dynamic may be effectively directed towards sound decisions.[18]

Those above considerations open up much of close concern for further contemplation, indicating where IE could carefully play an important role.

RANGING FURTHER

Alternative options are preferable, and IE can offer them. In relation to contemporary world affairs, 'psycho-paralysis' is perhaps a better phrase to adopt to characterise the present exasperating conditions of 'gridlock' in relation to thinking and actually manifested expressions of power. This is particularly the case in the currently angst-ridden West with its many tactical and operationally impacting distractions.[19]

All of these distractions and disruptive events and developments are unfolding during continued periods of contemporary 'strategic paucities' that befuddle potential grander movements on more liberal footings, and as more stringent and poisonous approaches instead fill gaps and normative to value vacuums much more exploitatively.[20] Current, jittery nerves need both calming and better holding, with more suitable footwear being found for hiking the hot, rocky roads anticipated ahead. As prevailing disruption can lead towards creativity in some circumstances—particularly in relation to how we deal with that disruption, citing the so-called disruption dilemma—alternate more laid-back conditions of drift and denial instead become increasingly unfeasible as the future rapidly unfolds.[21] Remaining passive and neglecting proactive IE concepts brings great risks. Indeed, IE can viably address potentially damaging laissez-faire policies.

WHERE NEXT?

IE can take us far. As suggested in this book, when confronting conditions of (1) globalised strategic risk, (2) complex co-existence plurality, (3) conducting multifunctional and special operations (MFOs-SOs/SpecOps), (4) navigating 'multiplexity', or (5) negotiating any combination of the above to differing degrees[22]—the IE concept arguably heralds much promise for several different decision-makers, stakeholders, and operatives. As also demonstrated, the different aspects of IE possess sufficiently empowering multi-scaler scope for their extended uptake. Both now and in the future, these aspects will require greater and more refined harnessing.[23] Simultaneously engaging in—at least approaches towards—greater IE professionalisation heralds dividends.[24]

IE GOING FORWARD

Chapters 3 and 4 of this book, in particular, offer a series of arguably viable IE roadmaps. These are expressed in the form of semistructured, multistep processes, frameworks, methodologies, and approaches. In all of their interconnectedness and interactivity, they have a rich, multi-adaptable potential for being seized and, thereby equipped, for practitioners to both employ and deploy IE-relevant constructs and pathways forward on suitably controlled bases. Naturally, due to the prevailing complexities involved, IE is not perfect nor should it ever completely be expected to be so because IE cannot exist without all of its discernible shortcomings and limitations.

However, if we delineate and are cognisant of its imperfections, feasible IE operational parameters become clearer. We thereby gain further insights as to

how better future design and architectural shaping can occur, both operationally and strategically. These signifiers furthermore suggest the directions IE
should take in the future with regard to subsequent and consequent actions,
which includes suitable acknowledgement towards those areas deserving
of further consideration in terms of their potential implications and impact-
related ramifications.[25] As has been remarked elsewhere, 'appropriate use
of models requires a good dose of common sense and an awareness of the
limitations of whatever model you happen to be using'.[26] High degrees of
fine-tuned pragmatism should persist in the IE context.

FINAL CONSIDERATIONS

Today, many IE-related tools, toolboxes, and toolsets are available. These
devices, so packaged and collectively encompassed by IE, are then ready
for judicious selection and use by practitioners, depending on the specific
environments encountered. This includes the specificities of the environments in which the practitioners are embedded and that they experience, both
directly and indirectly. As the local and global increasingly merge—mediated
by increasingly sophisticated and miniaturised technology held in the hands
of thereby empowered individuals—concepts such as *glocalisation* figure
prominently as more than just abstractions. We can expect both positive and
negative effects and outcomes. The presence of these alone demonstrates
where IE has an important role to perform as an alternatively empowering
navigator and negotiator.

In an era that demands substantial creativity, agility, flexibility, and interoperability across the full-spectrum of intelligence, defence, and security
enterprises—including all of their attendant activities, such as military, policing, and law enforcement–associated operations—IE stands out positively
as a progressive approach to adopt. It offers useful pathways to follow into
a quickly developing future, offering greater strategic-ranging vision and
operationally relevant adjustment guides.[27]

Indeed, at a minimum, the adoption of IE-related thinking requires
encouragement. This is especially important when risk-management-
drenched 'solution-fashioning', 'trouble-shooting', and 'problem-solving'
approaches are grasped by practitioners and operatives during the course
of rapidly unfolding activities. These approaches, in turn, belong to substantially demanding and resource-costly 'just-in-time' crisis and emergency management and first-responder associated 'fire-fighting', while
conditions of 'multiplexity' likewise feature. We need to carefully avoid
becoming overwhelmed.[28]

CLOSING REMARKS

Failure to adapt is a shortcoming. Today, it is necessary to address (1) immediate, short-term drivers largely originating in 'bottom-up' ways to (2) often domineering 'crisis management' approaches. This calls for the implementation of extended, judicious balancing, with 'top-down', longer-term, strategic management approaches. Otherwise, increasingly, other, potentially more negative, agendas will instead continue to prevail, and we will either narrow or lose through forfeiting our scope for greater advantageous opportunities. The risk remains prominent that we may instead be 'led up the garden path', or in other words, deceived to a substantial extent. Episodes like these can only be unhelpful at best and detrimental at worst, especially if they occur frequently. Moderate haste must succeed.

Both qualitatively and quantitatively, IE provides a highly useful guide to aid us on the journeys ahead. Problem-solving and trouble-shooting cannot merely be postponed, outsourced, or, more classically, 'muddled through'. Otherwise, 'blowback' is the dominant theme.[29] Even the most subjective situations need to be dealt with as objectively as possible. Therein lies another significant and persistent IE challenge, which tempers implementation when we are increasingly operating beyond the conventional.

Going forward, the intelligence theorist can learn much from the intelligence engineer, and vice versa. Simultaneously, intelligence professionals as 'scholar-practitioners' can better organise and unite over the whole course of their improved intelligence and operational endeavours to enterprises.[30] On attainable bases, IE provides viable alternatives to all problems looking like nails and to all solutions then being hammers. Equally, IE instead better equips anyone trying to 'eat soup with a knife'. IE gives us the essential innovation we need, and fast.

NOTES

1. See also A. Zegart and S.D. Krasner, eds., *Pragmatic Engagement amidst Global Uncertainty* (Washington, DC: Hoover Institution, 11 December 2015); F. Osinga, 'Organizing for insecurity and chaos', ch. 3 in R. Beeres et al., eds., *NL ARMS Netherlands Annual Review of Military Studies 2016* (The Hague, Netherlands: Asser/Springer, 2016), pp. 43–73; see also the creation of structures and mechanisms, e.g., in J.E. Barnes, 'EU defense ministers back new group focused on "hybrid warfare"', *Wall Street Journal* (19 May 2016), which includes liaison links to NATO (based on information from a non-attributable source).

2. Similar approaches and thinking are in A.D.M. Svendsen, 'The globalization of intelligence since 9/11: The optimization of intelligence liaison arrangements', *In-*

ternational Journal of Intelligence and CounterIntelligence, 21, 4 (December 2008), pp. 661–78.

3. For constructivism with regard to intelligence, especially as discussed in A.D.M. Svendsen, 'Connecting intelligence and theory', *Intelligence and National Security*, 24, 5 (October 2009), p. 711, p. 713, p. 715, pp. 720–23.

4. A.D.M. Svendsen, *Understanding the Globalization of Intelligence* (Basingstoke, UK: Palgrave Macmillan, 2012), p. 116 (emphasis added); see also as discussed and referenced in chapter 2.

5. See, e.g., as demonstrated with intelligence liaison in A.D.M. Svendsen, 'International intelligence liaison: A primer', *Romanian Journal of Intelligence Studies* (2016).

6. Svendsen, 'Connecting intelligence and theory', esp. p. 728.

7. See, e.g., many of the operating and strategic environments characterised in this study; T.X. Hammes, 'The end of globalization? The international security implications', *War on the Rocks* (2 August 2016); T.X. Hammes, 'Will technological convergence reverse globalization?' U.S. National Defense University—Strategic Forum (July 2016); J. Stiglitz, 'Globalization and its new discontents', *Strategist* (8 August 2016).

8. See, e.g., M. Hall, 'Former head of MI6 threatens to expose secrets of Iraq "dodgy dossier"', *Daily Telegraph* (21 July 2013); S. Aftergood, 'Dozens of leak referrals sent to DoJ each year', *FAS Secrecy News* (26 July 2016); P. Rosenzweig, 'More DNC leaks', *Lawfare*; 'Submarine data leak roils three governments', *Defense News* (13/26 August 2016); for more methodological insights, see '"Poacher" or 'fellow-gamekeeper"? Researching intelligence and liaison; accounting for wider general intelligence cooperation trends', chapter 3 of A.D.M. Svendsen, *The Professionalization of Intelligence Cooperation* (Basingstoke, UK: Palgrave Macmillan, 2012); C. Moran, *Company Confessions: Revealing CIA Secrets* (London: Biteback, 2015); C. Drew, 'Ex-SEAL member who wrote book on Bin Laden raid forfeits $6.8 Million', *New York Times* (19 August 2016).

9. Svendsen, *Understanding the Globalization of Intelligence*, p. 63; A.D.M. Svendsen, *Intelligence Cooperation and the War on Terror* (London: Routledge, 2010), esp. pp. 53–54, p. 65, p. 103, p. 121, p. 125, pp. 138–40, p. 155, pp. 157–58; on the 'politicisation' of intelligence from these and similar contexts, see P. F. Walsh, *Intelligence and Intelligence Analysis* (London: Routledge, 2011), p. 329, col. 1; 'Iraq inquiry: Why has the report taken so long?' BBC (9 May 2016); 'Iraq inquiry: Timeline of key moments', BBC (29 October 2015); G. Corera, 'The intelligence questions for Chilcot'; L. Kuenssberg, 'Chilcot report: Crystal clear, polite—But damning' and 'Chilcot report: Findings at-a-glance', BBC (4/6 July 2016); P. Sands, 'A grand and disastrous deceit', *London Review of Books*, 38, 15 (July 2016); S. Harris and N. Youssef, 'ISIS intel was cooked, House panel finds', *The Daily Beast*, J. Gould, 'House GOP probe: Central Command skewed ISIS-fight intel', *Defense News*, M. Ryan, 'House Republicans find Centcom produced overly upbeat intelligence on Islamic State', *Washington Post*; 'Initial findings of the U.S. House of Representatives Joint Task Force on U.S. Central Command Intelligence Analysis', *Small Wars Journal* (10–11/21 August 2016); A.D.M. Svendsen, 'Developing international

intelligence liaison against Islamic State', *International Journal of Intelligence and CounterIntelligence*, 29, 2 (2016), pp. 260–77; see also essays introduced by S. Marrin, 'Revisiting intelligence and policy: Problems with politicization and receptivity', *Intelligence and National Security*, 28, 1 (2013), pp. 1–4; 'Michael Hayden: Blame intel agencies, not White House, for getting Iraq wrong', NPR (23 February 2016); G. Packer, 'Can you keep a secret?' *New Yorker* (7 March 2016); 'Germany extols Turkish security cooperation to ease row over Islamists', Reuters (18 August 2016).

10. 'Politicisation' also is not always negative all of the time—see Svendsen, *Understanding the Globalization of Intelligence*, p. 148, for general 'politicisation' discussion refs, p. 237 col. 2; Svendsen, *The Professionalization of Intelligence Cooperation*, p. 243 col. 1; see also 'Gerald Ford White House altered Rockefeller Commission Report in 1975; Removed section on CIA assassination plots', *National Security Archive* (29 February 2016).

11. Svendsen, *Understanding the Globalization of Intelligence*, p. 63; see also examples suggested by M. Fetouri, 'Five years on, predictions by Gadhafi's son come true', *Al-Monitor* (28 February 2016); 'Islamic State "document haul" probed by German police', BBC (10 March 2016).

12. Svendsen, *The Professionalization of Intelligence Cooperation*, pp. 151–52, p. 155; Svendsen, *Understanding the Globalization of Intelligence*, pp. 127–32, p. 152; G. Hogan, 'Contestability: The key to more successful intelligence analysis', *Strategist* (4 August 2016); UK MoD, *Red Teaming Guide* (Shrivenham, UK: DCDC, 2013 [2nd ed.]), esp. pp. 3.9–3.11 (fig. 3.5 and table 3.1); for 'enterprise-thinking' and future sustainability, see A. Corrin, 'Intel community looks to life after TPED', C4ISRNet; and 'Pentagon awards HP Enterprise $443 million technology contract', Reuters (16/21 April 2016); 'Symantec results, forecast boosted by strong enterprise demand', Reuters (4 August 2016).

13. See, e.g., R. Heuer, *Psychology of Intelligence Analysis* (Washington, DC: CIA CSI, 1999); see also this dimension of intelligence in Svendsen, *Understanding the Globalization of Intelligence*, p. 7; other insights in E. Reynolds, 'Uncertainty can "cause more stress" than pain itself', *Wired*; and A. Elkus, 'Read my mind: Why it's hard to see things from the enemy's point of view', *War on the Rocks* (29/31 March 2016); C. Tripodi, 'Chilcot: The lessons of Iraq vs the reality of interventions', *Defence-in-Depth* (29 July 2016); Svendsen, *Understanding the Globalization of Intelligence*, p. 22; D. Kahneman, *Thinking, Fast and Slow* (London: Allen Lane, 2011).

14. On 'groupthink', see Svendsen, *Intelligence Cooperation and the War on Terror*, p. 22, p. 60, p. 96, p. 104, pp. 116–17, p. 169; Svendsen, *Understanding the Globalization of Intelligence*, p. 22, p. 56, p. 112, p. 128, p. 151; Svendsen, *The Professionalization of Intelligence Cooperation*, p. 137, pp. 142–43, pp. 150–53.

15. Abstract quoted from A. Mintz and C. Wayne, 'The polythink syndrome and elite group decision-making', *Political Psychology*, 37 (2016), pp. 3–21; G. Kenyon, 'The man who studies the spread of ignorance', BBC Future (6 January 2016).

16. For benchmarking concepts, see Svendsen, *Understanding the Globalization of Intelligence*, p. 66; and Svendsen, *The Professionalization of Intelligence Cooperation*, p. 7.

17. Mintz and Wayne, 'The polythink syndrome and elite group decision-making' (emphasis added).

18. *Ibid.*; see also M.J. Mazarr, *Rethinking Risk in National Security* (Basingstoke, UK: Palgrave Macmillan, 2016); D. Wagner and D. Disparte, *Global Risk Agility and Decision Making* (London: Springer, 2016); S. Winnefeld, M. Morell, and S. Vinograd, 'Opinion: U.S. should adopt interest-based approach to national security', *USNI News*; M.V. Hayden, 'Opinion: What intelligence briefings can tell us about candidates', *New York Times* (4/10 August 2016).

19. See, e.g., J. Dempsey, 'Munich hosts a beleaguered West'; N. Barkin, 'Follow the leader? Germany struggles as Syria, refugee crises rage', Reuters; J. Dempsey, 'Can the West regain its influence?'; 'The West's self-imposed powerlessness', *Carnegie Europe*; D. Dehez, 'Germany and Russia: Berlin's deadly self-delusions', *War on the Rocks*; B. Jones, 'The rising powers: A mixed bag for the international order', Brookings Institution (12–13/15/20 February 2016); E. Donahoe, 'So software has eaten the world: What does it mean for human rights, security and governance?' *Just Security* (18 March 2016); D. Lee, 'US ready to "hand over" the Internet's naming system', BBC (18 August 2016); M. Galeotti, 'Hybrid, ambiguous, and non-linear? How new is Russia's "new way of war"?' *Small Wars & Insurgencies*, 27, 2 (2016), pp. 282–301; M. Bhagavan, 'Not just Trump: The chilling rise in global authoritarianism', *Defense One*; D. Benaim and P. Cammack, 'How Trumpism went global', *New Republic* (21 March 2016); D. Barno and N. Bensahel, 'A new generation of unrestricted warfare', *War on the Rocks*; J. Techau, 'Sophisticated states are failing', *Carnegie Europe*, R. Emmott, 'Russia warns U.S. over naval incident as NATO tensions laid bare', Reuters; E. Schmitt, 'Russia bolsters its submarine fleet, and tensions with U.S. rise', *New York Times*; S. Biddle and J. Shapiro, 'America can't do much about ISIS', *Defense One*, 'The collapse of Syria's ceasefire?' Soufan Group; J. Landay and P. Stewart, 'U.S. split deepens over Putin's intentions in Syria civil war'; 'China's Xi takes up new military title as part of reforms process', Reuters; I. Daalder and R. Kagan, 'The U.S. can't afford to end its global leadership role', *Washington Post*; A. Monaghan, 'No going back to business as usual for NATO and Russia', *Chatham House*; R. Rampton, 'In European tour Obama shows support for his closest allies', Reuters; E. Tomiuc, 'Obama calls for EU unity, more collective defense spending', Radio Free Europe/Radio Liberty; E. Fabry, 'Fear of TTIP, globalisation, or a middle class downgrade?' EurActiv.com; D. Twining, 'Trilateral bloc could defend a fraying liberal order', *USGMF* (19–29 April 2016); J. Cassidy, 'A Europe of Donald Trumps?' *New Yorker*; S. Hamid, 'Donald Trump and the authoritarian temptation', Brookings Institution (2/9 May 2016).

20. See also the concerns articulated in diverse sources, e.g., H. Strachan, *The Direction of War* (Cambridge: Cambridge University Press, 2013); R. Synovitz, 'Is Russia "weaponizing refugees" to advance its geopolitical goals?' Radio Free Europe/Radio Liberty; P. Taylor, 'EU's Tower of Babel may fall while leaders distracted', Reuters (19/29 February 2016); M. Urban, 'Europe's migrant story enters new phase', BBC (10 May 2016); I. Bremmer, 'The world is failing refugees from Nauru to the U.S.', *TIME*; D. Vincenti, 'New geopolitical crises demand a more dynamic EU neighbourhood policy', EurActiv.com; 'Japan, China, South Korea foreign ministers

to meet August 23–24', Reuters (16/22 August 2016); R. Seely, 'When is a cold war not a cold war?' *Defence-in-Depth Blog*; D. Chollet, 'In defense of the Obama Doctrine', *Defense One*; S. Coughlan, 'Tony Blair warns of "flabby liberalism"', BBC; J. Bittner, 'Can the European center hold?' *New York Times*; C. Lynch, 'Fearing Trump, U.N. embraces the art of the deal', *Foreign Policy* (9/13/22/24/28 March 2016); 'European divisions "hardening", warns German think tank', EurActiv.com (18 August 2016); L. Summers, 'What's behind the revolt against global integration?' *Washington Post* (10 April 2016); J. Gans, *The Disruption Dilemma* (Cambridge, MA: MIT Press, 2016); 'North Korea says it has resumed plutonium production—Report' and 'Japan, China, South Korea to urge North Korea to stop provocation', Reuters (17/24 August 2016); H. Cooper, 'Long emphasis on terror may hurt U.S. in conventional war, army chief says', *New York Times*; S. Engelberg, 'Why is America still saying "never again" about terrorism?' *ProPublica*; D. Tierney, 'Al-Qaeda's war on America just entered its third decade', *Atlantic* (15 May/19/23 August 2016); A. de Hoop Scheffer et al., 'The future of US global leadership', *Chatham House* (May 2016); W. Bowen, 'NATO and the challenges of implementing effective deterrence vis-à-vis Russia', *Defence-in-Depth Blog* (16 May 2016); E. Colby and J. Solomon, 'Facing Russia: Conventional defence and deterrence in Europe', *Survival*, 57, 6 (2015), pp. 21–50; S. Frühling and G. Lasconjarias, 'NATO, A2/AD and the Kaliningrad Challenge', *Survival*, 58, 2 (2016), pp. 95–116; I. Lesser, 'Turkey's travails, transatlantic consequences: Reflections on a recent visit', German Marshall Fund of the United States (24 May 2016); J. Lloyd, 'Commentary: Political decency is going to hell', Reuters (6 June 2016); S. Nakhoul and A.J. Yackley, 'Turkish president gains upper hand in power struggle'; W. Schomberg, 'UK seeks to assuage global worries over path to Brexit', Reuters (24 July 2016); R. Reeve and T. Street, 'Brexit: Whither UK defence and foreign policy?' *ORG Briefing* (July 2016); 'Britain says it needs constructive dialogue with Russia despite differences', Reuters (11 August 2016); K. Ven Bruusgaard, 'Russian strategic deterrence', *Survival*, 58, 4 (2016), pp. 7–26.

21. See as covered in detail in N. Gowing and C. Langdon, 'Want to lead? Then tear up the rulebook', *World Today* (June & July 2016), pp. 12–16; N. Gowing and C. Langdon, 'Thinking the unthinkable: A new imperative for leadership in the digital age', *CIMA Report* (May 2016); J. Lloyd, 'Commentary: The alchemy of political narcissism', Reuters (22 July 2016); J. Tlapa, 'Disrupt or be disrupted', *USNI Proceedings Magazine 142/8/1,362* (August 2016); K. Coleman, 'Regulations may impede change', C4ISRNet (23 August 2016); Gans, *The Disruption Dilemma*; R. Cohen, 'Opinion: The Trump-Farage road show', *New York Times* (29 August 2016).

22. See, e.g., this concept as used in chapter 3; J. Kirkpatrick, 'Interview—Amitav Acharya', *e-IR.info* (April 2016); see also 'Massacre reports show U.S. inability to curb Iraq militias'; 'Iraq executions carried out without proper trial, fuelled by vengeance—U.N.'; 'As Kerry lands in Nigeria, air force says top Boko Haram fighters killed'; and 'Kerry tells Nigeria fight against Islamists is not just a military one', Reuters (23 August 2016).

23. See also, e.g., M. Olsen, 'The case for closing Guantanamo Bay', *Cipher Brief* (25 February 2016); B. Wittes, 'A big Guantanamo transfer: Progress towards the site's obsolescence', *Lawfare*; 'Biden says expects Guantanamo prison to close be-

fore Obama leaves office', Reuters (16/25 August 2016); see also efforts, e.g., K.M. Pollack, 'Security and public order'; B. Orino, 'Fresh ideas for the defense establishment, from emerging leaders', Brookings Institution (February/8 March 2016); C. Dickstein, 'Dunford: Changes needed to prepare for "dynamic and complex" future wars', *Stars and Stripes* (29 March 2016); 'Army building command post of the future', C4ISRNet (15 August 2016).

24. On intelligence and professionalisation, see Svendsen, *The Professionalization of Intelligence Cooperation*; see also J. Richards, 'Intelligence studies, academia and professionalization', *International Journal of Intelligence, Security, and Public Affairs*, 18, 1 (2016), pp. 20–33; E. Kleinsmith, 'Intelligence certifications: Coming an agency near you', *In Public Safety* (10 August 2016); J.A. Gentry, 'The "professionalization" of intelligence analysis: A skeptical perspective', *International Journal of Intelligence and CounterIntelligence*, 29, 4 (2016), pp. 643–76; M.E. Miller, 'Special operations forces and the professionalization of foreign internal defense', *Small Wars Journal* (24 August 2016).

25. For federation/system of systems-related limitations, see A.D.M. Svendsen, 'Advancing "defence-in-depth"', *Defense & Security Analysis*, 31, 1 (2015), p. 62, pp. 64–65; A.D.M. Svendsen, 'Contemporary intelligence innovation in practice', *Defence Studies*, 15, 2 (2015), pp. 109–10, pp. 113–14; Svendsen, *The Professionalization of Intelligence Cooperation*, pp. 135–62; for similar thinking and approaches, A. Svendsen, 'The globalization of intelligence since 9/11: Frameworks and operational parameters', *International Journal of Intelligence and CounterIntelligence*, 21, 1 (March 2008), pp. 129–44; see also the series of postings associated with J. Hudak, 'Shining light on explanatory journalism's impact on media, democracy, and society', Brookings Institution (24 February 2016); W. Pincus, 'Reflections on secrecy and the press from a life in journalism', *National Security, Technology, and Law—Hoover Institution, no. 1602* (2016); 'Don't count on technology to save you in a disaster—Researchers', Reuters (25 August 2016).

26. J.O. Weatherall, *The Physics of Finance—Predicting the Unpredictable* (London: Short Books, 2014), p. 206; F. Hill, 'Putin: The one-man show the West doesn't understand', *Bulletin of the Atomic Scientists*, 72, 3 (2016), pp. 140–44; 'Kremlin to NATO—Resurgent Russia not a threat, but will defend its interests', Reuters; M. Galeotti, 'The West needs to stop panicking about Russia's "hybrid" warfare', *Vox* (4–5 May 2016); R. Norton-Taylor, 'Britain is not at war with Russia, nor is it at peace', *Guardian* (19 May 2016); C. Coker, 'Rethinking strategy: NATO and the Warsaw Summit', Norwegian Institute of International Affairs (May 2016); 'Deputy secretary general: NATO ideally equipped to project stability beyond our borders', *NATO Update*; M. Banks, 'NATO members face hard budget choices, official says', *Defense News*; D. Dyomkin, 'Putin says Romania, Poland may now be in Russia's cross-hairs', Reuters (23/26/28 May 2016); T. Snyder, 'The wars of Vladimir Putin', *New York Review of Books*; and S.J. Freedberg, Jr., 'Reach out to Russia: Former EU-COM Breedlove', *Breaking Defense* (9 June 2016); T. Gibbons-Neff, 'NATO to send "combat-ready" battalions near Russian border', *Washington Post*, G. Jean, 'Canadian frigate encountered "heavy Russian presence" in Black Sea', IHS Jane's 360; 'Russian military drills check mobilization readiness', Associated Press; M. Eckel, 'Former

U.S. ambassadors spar over Russia, NATO, Ukraine'; and 'Lithuania steps up defenses', Radio Free Europe/Radio Liberty (14–15 June 2016); J. Dempsey, 'Strategic Europe: Is NATO taking on more than it can chew?' *Carnegie Europe*; P. Coyer, 'The flashpoint no one is talking about: The Black Sea', *Forbes*; S.J. Freedberg, Jr., 'NATO not ready as Russian sub threat rises: CSIS', *Breaking Defense* (9/23/25 July 2016); 'NATO's foothold in Eastern Med is faltering', Lexington Institute; G. Gotev and J. Schalit, 'US moves nuclear weapons from Turkey to Romania', EurActiv.com (16/18 August 2016); 'With Biden visit, U.S. seeks balance with truculent Turkey', Reuters; 'Syria war: US warns over Turkish-Kurdish violence', BBC; 'Turkey's army digs deeper into Syria', EurActiv.com (23/29 August 2016); W. Pincus, 'Do facts and logic count in Donald Trump's world?'; 'Intelligence briefings for candidates have become a political football'; N. Toosi, 'Trump makes intel community queasy', *Politico*; M. Sulick, 'Russia's checkered history of intelligence sharing with the U.S', *Cipher Brief* (26 July/17/10 August 2016); J. Marcus, 'Are Russia's military advances a problem for NATO?' BBC; 'Putin hints at war in Ukraine but may be seeking diplomatic edge', Reuters (11/16 August 2016); A. Barnard and A.E. Kramer, 'Iran revokes Russia's use of air base, saying Moscow "betrayed trust"', *New York Times*, A. Stent, 'Why there will be no "reset" with Russia', Brookings Institution; 'Finland and Sweden's proposed military co-operation with US likely to trigger limited Russian military response', IHS Jane's 360 (22/24 August 2016); 'NATO: Russia increasingly staging snap military drills', Associated Press; 'The limits of U.S. influence in Syria', Soufan Group (29–30 August 2016).

27. See also 'Civil war, cybersecurity, and climate change', Soufan Group; B. Jentleson, 'American power in the rearview mirror and on the road ahead', *War on the Rocks* (18 August 2016); R.J. Lempert, 'Infrastructure design must change with climate', Rand Corporation (12 August 2016).

28. See, e.g., A.D.M. Svendsen, 'Sharpening SOF tools, their strategic use and direction', *Defence Studies*, 14, 3 (2014); Svendsen, *Understanding the Globalization of Intelligence*, p. 107, p. 126, pp. 129–30; Svendsen, *The Professionalization of Intelligence Cooperation*, p. 37; see also 'survival approaches' in, e.g., D. Inserra, 'Preparing for the worst: How to respond to an active shooter', *Daily Signal* (26 July 2016); more widely, A. Macdonald, 'New tans, same old "polycrisis" as Europe's summer ends', Reuters (29 August 2016).

29. Svendsen, *Understanding the Globalization of Intelligence*, pp. 72–73, pp. 130–31, p. 147, on 'muddling', p. 107; A.D.M. Svendsen, 'Strategy and disproportionality in contemporary conflicts', *Journal of Strategic Studies*, 33, 3 (June 2010), p. 385; Svendsen, *The Professionalization of Intelligence Cooperation*, p. 10, from p. 119, p. 123, p. 162; J.A. Mendosa, 'Operations-driven intelligence: Is the shirt on backwards?', *International Journal of Intelligence and CounterIntelligence*, 29, 4 (2016), pp. 677–99; J. Andrews, *The World in Conflict* (London: Economist/Profile, 2015); B. Stewart, 'Analysis: Cold war–style hotline proposed as tension between East-West rises in Ukraine', CBC News (30 April 2016); E. Thomas, 'Why we need a foreign policy elite', *New York Times*, S. Watts, 'How the U.S. can better help militaries around the world', *Lawfare*; 'A generation of Syrian children who don't count', Reuters (3–4 May 2016); M. Bishara, 'Opinion: America's war for the Greater

Middle East', *Al Jazeera* (4 August 2016); N. Sagener, 'Organization for Security and Co-operation in Europe: More international cooperation needed', EurActiv.com (2 June 2016); Gowing and Langdon, 'Want to lead? Then tear up the rulebook'; Gowing and Langdon 'Thinking the unthinkable'; M. Garavoglia, 'After the emergency: What European migration policy will eventually look like', Brookings Institution (27 July 2016); P. Apps, 'Commentary: Is Vladimir Putin deliberately destabilizing U.S. politics?'; J. Menn, D. Volz and M. Hosenball, 'FBI probes hacking of Democratic congressional group—Sources', Reuters (26/28–29 July 2016); 'Putin, Erdogan vow new era of close relations', Radio Free Europe/Radio Liberty; E. Toksabay and T. gumrukcu, 'EU making "serious mistakes" over failed Turkish coup: Turkish minister'; M. Kambas and A. Bronic, 'Out of sight, out of mind? Europe's migrant crisis still simmers', Reuters (9/10 August 2016); D. Trenin, 'Russia and NATO must communicate better', Carnegie Moscow; J. Kitfield, '"Our greatest challenge": CJCS Gen. Dunford', *Breaking Defense*, A. Gabuev and G. Shtraks, 'China's one belt, one road initiative and the Sino-Russian entente'; D. Trenin, 'Is Russia safe from extremist attacks like those in Europe?' Carnegie Moscow; A.K. Yildirim, 'Turkey's impending Eastern turn', *Sada-CEIP*; L. Lakhani, 'Russia-Iran alliance: Shifting the power dynamic', *Cipher Brief*, J. Judson, 'Syring on threats: "The game has been escalated"', *Defense News*, 'Turkish PM says to put intelligence agencies under umbrella structure' and 'Turkey to take more active role on Syria in next six months, PM says'; 'Putin to meet May, Merkel, Hollande and Erdogan in China', Reuters (8/9/12/17/18/20/30 August 2016).

30. Richards, 'Intelligence studies, academia and professionalization', pp. 20–33; S. Foerster and R. Raymond, 'Balanced internationalism: 5 core principles to guide U.S. national security policy', *National Interest* (31 July 2016).

Appendix

IE-Mapping Templates

Advanced Intelligence Analysis + Engineering - AIAE
Mapping Sheet #1
Overall 'Situational Awareness' Evaluation (SoSA/G-J2)
CONTEXT APPRECIATION - Observe + Orient

System attributes/ variables > e.g. inc. captures + covers...? > --------- SoSA units (e.g. PMESII):	Internal influences / factors 'Who?' / 'Which?'	Rationale 'Why?'	Types + Forms 'What?'	Conditions + Terms 'When?'	Trends (+ dynamics/ flows) 'Where?'	Functions 'How?'	External influences / factors 'Who?' / 'Which?'	Effects + Outcomes 'What?' / 'S.W.O.T.'
Political (inc. law/legislation)								
Military								
Economic								
Social (inc. sociological + cultural)								
Informational/ Intelligence (inc. technological)								
Infrastructural (inc. environment[al])								

Adam D.M. Svendsen, PhD

Figure A.1.   IE Mapping Template #1
Courtesy of the Author

Advanced Intelligence Analysis + Engineering - AIAE
Mapping Sheet #2
Overall 'Mission Accomplishment' Guide (SoSE/G-J3)
SOLUTION FASHIONING - Decide + Act

SoSA units (e.g. PMESII) > ---- 'Levels' (of interactivity/ implementation/ engineering):	Political (inc. law/ legislation)	Military	Economic	Social (inc. sociological + cultural)	Informational/ Intelligence (inc. technological)	Infrastructural (inc. environment[al])
Ideological (e.g. Ideas/Why realise?)						
Theoretical (e.g. Aspirations/Why do?)						
Strategic (e.g. Directions/How go?)						
Policy (e.g. Aims/Where go?)						
Operational (e.g. How/What realise?)						
Tactical (e.g. How/What do?)						Privacy
Individual (as 'professional') (e.g. What/Which realise?)						buffer
Personal (e.g. Who do?)						

Adam D.M. Svendsen, PhD

Figure A.2.   IE Mapping Template #2
Courtesy of the Author

Advanced Intelligence Analysis + Engineering - AIAE
Mapping Sheet #3
Fusion grid = mapping System Attributes/Variables + Levels
for each specified SoS unit of analysis* - e.g. using PMESII model: Political; Military; Economic; Social; Informational/Intelligence; Infrastructural (*show which is selected for focus)

System Attributes/ Variables> ---- 'Levels' (of interactivity/ implementatio n/engineering):	Internal influences / factors 'Who?' / 'Which?'	Rationale 'Why?'	Types + Forms 'What?'	Conditions + Terms 'When?'	Trends (+ dynamics/ flows) 'Where?'	Functions 'How?'	External influences / factors 'Who?' / 'Which?'	Effects + Outcomes 'What?' / 'S.W.O.T.'
Ideological (e.g. Ideas/Why realise?)								
Theoretical (e.g. Aspirations/Why do?)								
Strategic (e.g. Directions/How go?)								
Policy (e.g. Aims/Where go?)								
Operational (e.g. How/What realise?)								
Tactical (e.g. How/What do?)								Privacy
Individual (as 'professional') (e.g. What/Which realise?)								buffer
Personal (e.g. Who do?)								

Adam D.M. Svendsen, PhD

Figure A.3.   IE Mapping Template #3
Courtesy of the Author

Advanced Intelligence Analysis + Engineering - AIAE
Mapping Sheet #4

OVERVIEW SNAPSHOT SUMMARY
At a minimum for context consider + fuse:

(A) 'Key Actors' - e.g. who? (e.g. OC groups, individuals, other 'targets', etc.)	**(A1) Events** - e.g. what? when? where?
	(A2) Patterns - e.g. how?
	(A3) Drivers - e.g. why?
(B) 'forces/factors of change' - e.g. what activity? (e.g. SOC areas, etc.)	**(B1) Events** - e.g. what? when? where?
	(B2) Patterns - e.g. how?
	(B3) Drivers - e.g. why?
(C) 'possible change over time' - e.g. when? / where? (e.g. environment, PESTLE/PMESII [SoSD] indicators, SWOT, etc.)	**(C1) Events** - e.g. what? when? where?
	(C2) Patterns - e.g. how?
	(C3) Drivers - e.g. why?

Aim = capture: (i) the **players**; (ii) their **relationships**; (iii) their **drivers** (e.g. their means, motives & opportunities).

Adam D.M. Svendsen, PhD

Figure A.4. IE Mapping Template #4
Courtesy of the Author

Select Bibliography

Agrell, W., and G.F. Treverton. 2009. 'The science of intelligence: Reflections on a field that never was', ch. 11 in Agrell, W., and G.F. Treverton, eds., *National Intelligence Systems* (Cambridge: Cambridge University Press).

———. 2015. *National Intelligence and Science: Beyond the Great Divide in Analysis and Policy* (Oxford: Oxford University Press).

Aldrich, R.J., and R. Cormac. 2016. *The Black Door: Spies, Secret Intelligence and British Prime Ministers* (London: Collins).

Aldrich, R.J., and J. Kasuku. 2012. 'Escaping from American intelligence: Culture, ethnocentrism and the Anglosphere', *International Affairs*, 88, 5 (September).

Aldrich, R.J., W.K. Wark, and C. Andrew, eds. 2016. *Secret Intelligence: A Reader*, 2nd ed. (London: Routledge).

Amerson, K., and S.B. Meredith, III. 2016. 'The future operating environment 2050: Chaos, complexity and competition', *Small Wars Journal* (31 July).

Anderson, QC, D. 2015. *A Question of Trust: Report of the Investigatory Powers Review* (June).

———. 2016. *Report of the Bulk Powers Review* (August).

Andrew, C. 2004. 'Intelligence analysis needs to look backwards before looking forward', *History and Policy* (1 June).

Andrews, J. 2015. *The World in Conflict: Understanding the World's Troublespots* (London: Economist/Profile Books).

Ansoff, H.I. 1975. 'Managing strategic surprise by response to weak signals', *California Management Review*, 18, 2, pp. 21–33.

Arcos, R., and R. Pherson, eds. 2015. *Intelligence Communication in the Digital Era: Transforming Security, Defence and Business* (Basingstoke, UK: Palgrave Macmillan).

Avery, E.J., M. Graham, and S. Park. 2016. 'Planning makes (closer to) perfect: exploring United States' local government officials' evaluations of crisis management', *Journal of Contingencies and Crisis Management*.

119

Ayoub, K., and K. Payne. 2015. 'Strategy in the age of artificial intelligence', *Journal of Strategic Studies* (November).

Barlow, M., and G. Fell. 2016. *Patrolling the Dark Net: What You Don't Know Will Hurt You* (London: O'Reilly).

Barnes, A. 2015. 'Making intelligence analysis more intelligent: Using numeric probabilities', *Intelligence and National Security*.

Bartlett, J. 2014. *The Dark Net* (London: Windmill).

BASIC. 2016. 'The 2016 Nuclear Security Summit returns to Washington', *BASIC–British American Security Information Council Report* (24 March).

Beebe, S.M., and R.H. Pherson. 2012. *Cases in Intelligence Analysis: Structured Analytic Techniques in Action* (Washington, DC: CQ Press).

Bergstein, B. 2016. 'Head of British intelligence agency on Apple, Snowden, and regrets', *MIT Technology Review* (11 March).

Betts, R.K. 1978. 'Analysis, war, and decision: Why intelligence failures are inevitable', *World Politics*, 31, 1 (October), pp. 61–89.

———. 2009. *Enemies of Intelligence: Knowledge and Power in American National Security* (New York: Columbia University Press).

Bhuta, N., S. Beck, R. Geiβ, H-Y. Liu, and C. Kreβ, eds. 2016. *Autonomous Weapons Systems: Law, Ethics, Policy* (Cambridge: Cambridge University Press).

Blockley, D. 2012. *Engineering: A Very Short Introduction* (Oxford: Oxford University Press).

Borgman, C.L. 2015. *Big Data, Little Data, No Data* (Cambridge, MA: MIT Press).

Bowen, W., M. Moran, and D. Esfandiary. 2016. *Living on the Edge: Iran and the Practice of Nuclear Hedging* (Basingstoke, UK: Palgrave Macmillan).

Bowyer, R. 2004. *Campaign Dictionary of Military Terms*, 3rd ed. (Oxford: Macmillan).

Bukkvoll, T. 2016. 'Russian special operations forces in Crimea and Donbas', *Parameters*, 46, 2, pp. 13–21.

Bułhak, W., and T. Wegener Friis, eds. 2014. *Need To Know: Eastern and Western Perspectives* (Odense: University Press of Southern Denmark).

Bunnik, A., A. Cawley, M. Mulqueen, and A. Zwitter, eds. 2016. *Big Data Challenges: Society, Security, Innovation and Ethics* (Basingstoke, UK: Palgrave Pivot).

Burdick, A. et al. 2012. *Digital_Humanities* (Cambridge, MA: MIT Press).

Burgess, A., A. Alemanno, and J. Zinn, eds. 2016. *Routledge Handbook of Risk Studies* (London: Routledge).

Burke, J. 2016. *The New Threat From Islamic Militancy* (London: Vintage).

Burrows, M. 2014. *The Future, Declassified* (Basingstoke, UK: Palgrave Macmillan).

Byman, D., and M. Kroenig. 2016. 'Reaching beyond the ivory tower: A "how to" manual', *Security Studies*, 25, 2, pp. 289–319.

Campbell, M. 2016. 'How Congress can prevent a nuclear Iran', *Georgetown Security Studies Review* (15 May).

Carter, J.G., D.L. Carter, S. Chermak, and E. McGarrell. 2016. 'Law enforcement fusion centers: Cultivating an information sharing environment while safeguarding privacy', *Journal of Police and Criminal Psychology* (May).

Chandler, D. 2014. *Resilience: The Governance of Complexity* (London: Routledge).

Chesterman, S. 2010. 'Privacy and surveillance in the age of terror', *Survival*, 52, 5, pp. 31–46.

———. 2011. *One Nation Under Surveillance* (Oxford: Oxford University Press).

CISC. 2007. 'Strategic early warning for criminal intelligence: Theoretical framework and sentinel methodology', *Criminal Intelligence Service Canada* (Ottawa, ON: Criminal Intelligence Service Canada, Central Bureau).

Clark, R.M. 2012. *Intelligence Analysis: A Target-Centric Approach*, 4th ed. (Washington, DC: CQ Press).

———. 2013. *Intelligence Collection* (Washington, DC: CQ Press).

Clark, R.M., and W.L. Mitchell. 2015. *Target-Centric Network Modeling: Case Studies in Analyzing Complex Intelligence Issues* (Washington, DC: CQ Press).

Clauser, J., and J. Goldman. 2008. *An Introduction to Intelligence Research and Analysis* (Lanham, MD: Scarecrow Press).

CLTC. 2016. 'CLTC Scenarios', *CLTC—Center for Long-term Cybersecurity*. University of California, Berkeley (April).

Coker, C. 2016. 'Rethinking strategy: NATO and the Warsaw Summit', *Norwegian Institute of International Affairs* (May).

Colby, E., and J. Solomon. 2015. 'Facing Russia: Conventional defence and deterrence in Europe', *Survival*, 57, 6, pp. 21–50.

Connable, B. 2012. *Military Intelligence Fusion for Complex Operations: A New Paradigm* (Washington, DC: Rand Corporation).

Corera, G. 2015. *Intercept: The Secret History of Computers and Spies* (London: Weidenfeld & Nicolson).

Corman, S.R. 2016. 'The narrative rationality of violent extremism', *Social Science Quarterly*, 97, pp. 9–18.

Coulthart, S. 2016. 'Why do analysts use structured analytic techniques? An in-depth study of an American intelligence agency', *Intelligence and National Security* (March).

Czuperski, M., E. Higgins, F. Hof, B. Nimmo, and J.E. Herbst. 2016. *Distract Deceive Destroy: Putin at War in Syria* (Washington, DC: Atlantic Council).

Dahl, E.J. 2013. *Intelligence and Surprise Attack: Failure and Success from Pearl Harbor to 9/11 and Beyond* (Washington, DC: Georgetown University Press).

Danchev, A. 2016. *On Good and Evil and the Grey Zone* (Edinburgh: Edinburgh University Press).

Davies, P.H.J. 2012. *Intelligence and Government in Britain and the United States: A Comparative Perspective* (Westport, CT: Praeger Security International).

———. 2016. 'The problem of defence intelligence', *Intelligence and National Security*.

Davies, P.H.J., and K.C. Gustafson, eds. 2013. *Intelligence Elsewhere: Spies and Espionage outside the Anglosphere* (Washington, DC: Georgetown University Press).

De Graaff, B., and J.M. Nyce with C. Locke. 2016. *Handbook of European Intelligence Cultures* (Lanham, MD: Rowman & Littlefield).

De Hoop Scheffer, A. et al. 2016. 'The future of US global leadership: Implications for Europe, Canada and transatlantic cooperation', *Chatham House Research Paper* (May).

Degaut, M. 2015. 'Spies and policymakers: Intelligence in the information age', *Intelligence and National Security*.

Dover, R., and M.S. Goodman, eds. 2011. *Learning from the Secret Past: Cases in British Intelligence History* (Washington, DC: Georgetown University Press).

Dover, R., M.S. Goodman, and C. Hillebrand. eds. 2013. *Routledge Companion to Intelligence Studies* (London: Routledge Companions).

Duggan, P. 2016. 'SOF's cyber fringe', *Small Wars Journal* (10 February).

Dupont, A., and W.J. Reckmeyer. 2012. 'Australia's national security priorities: Addressing strategic risk in a globalised world', *Australian Journal of International Affairs*, 66, 1.

Durch, W., J. Larik, and R. Ponzio. 2016. 'Just security and the crisis of global governance', *Survival*, 58, 4, pp. 95–112.

Duyvesteyn, I., B. de Jong, and J. van Reijn, eds. 2014. *The Future of Intelligence: Challenges in the 21st Century* (London: Routledge).

Eagle, N., and K. Greene. 2014. *Reality Mining: Data to Engineer a Better World* (Cambridge, MA: MIT Press).

Fägersten, B. 2014. 'European intelligence cooperation', ch. 8 in Duyvesteyn, de Jong and van Reijn, eds. *The Future of Intelligence*.

———. 2015. 'EU doesn't need a CIA—But better intelligence would help', EurActiv.com (16 October).

———. 2015. 'Intelligence and decision-making within the common foreign and security policy', *European Policy Analysis* (Stockholm: Swedish Institute for European Policy Studies, October).

———. 2016. 'For EU eyes only? Intelligence and European security', *EUISS Issue Brief* 8 (March).

Farwell, J.P. 2016. 'Victory in today's wars: New insights on the role of communications', *Parameters*, 46, 2, pp. 93–100.

Finegan, R. 2016. 'Shadowboxing in the dark: Intelligence and counter-terrorism in Northern Ireland', *Terrorism and Political Violence*, 28, 3, pp. 497–519.

Fisher, L. 2009. *The Perfect Swarm: The Science of Complexity in Everyday Life* (New York: Basic Books).

Fjäder, C. 2014. 'The nation-state, national security and resilience in the age of globalisation', *Resilience*, 2, 2, pp. 114–29.

Foot, M.R.D. 1978 (2013). *Six Faces of Courage* (London: Methuen/Pen & Sword).

Frühling, S., and G. Lasconjarias. 2016. 'NATO, A2/AD and the Kaliningrad challenge', *Survival*, 58, 2, pp. 95–116.

Fukuyama, F. 2016. 'Reflections on Chinese governance', *Journal of Chinese Governance*, 1, 3, pp. 379–91.

Galeotti, M. 2016. 'Hybrid, ambiguous, and non-linear? How new is Russia's "new way of war"?' *Small Wars & Insurgencies*, 27, 2, pp. 282–301.

Galliott, J., and W. Reed, eds. 2016. *Ethics and the Future of Spying: Technology, National Security and Intelligence Collection* (London: Routledge).

Gambetta, D., and S. Hertog. 2016. 'Uncivil engineers: The surprising link between education and jihad', *Foreign Affairs* (10 March).

Gans, J. 2016. *The Disruption Dilemma* (Cambridge, MA: MIT Press).

Gearon, L. 2015. 'Education, security and intelligence studies', *British Journal of Educational Studies*, 63, 3, pp. 263–79.

Gelles, M.G. 2016. *Insider Threat: Prevention, Detection, Mitigation, and Deterrence* (Oxford: Butterworth-Heinemann).

Gentry, J.A. 2016. 'The "professionalization" of intelligence analysis: A skeptical perspective', *International Journal of Intelligence and CounterIntelligence*, 29, 4, pp. 643–76.

George, R.Z. 2016. 'Intelligence and strategy', ch. 8 in J. Baylis, J.J. Wirtz, and C.S. Gray, eds. *Strategy in the Contemporary World*, 5th ed. (Oxford: Oxford University Press).

Gerber, T.P., and J. Zavisca. 2016. 'Does Russian propaganda work?' *Washington Quarterly*, 39, 2, pp. 79–98.

Glenny, M. 2011. *Dark Market: Cyberthieves, Cybercops and You* (London: Bodley Head).

Goldman, J., ed. 2005. *Ethics of Spying: A Reader for the Intelligence Professional* (Lanham, MD: Scarecrow Press).

Goldman, Z.K., and S.J. Rascoff, eds. 2016. *Global Intelligence Oversight: Governing Security in the Twenty-First Century* (Oxford: Oxford University Press).

Gompert, D.C., and M. Libicki. 2015. 'Waging cyber war the American way', *Survival*, 57, 4.

Goodman, M.S. 2015. 'Evolution of a relationship: The foundations of Anglo-American intelligence sharing', *CIA Studies in Intelligence*, 59, 2.

Gowing, N., and C. Langdon. 2016. 'Thinking the unthinkable: A new imperative for leadership in the digital age', *CIMA Report* (May).

Gowing, N., and C. Langdon. 2016. 'Want to lead? Then tear up the rulebook', *World Today* (June–July), pp. 12–16.

Greene Sands, R.R. 2016. *Assessing Special Operations Forces Language, Region, and Culture Needs: Leveraging Digital and LRC Learning to Reroute the "Roadmap" from Human Terrain to Human Domain* (MacDill AFB, FL: Joint Special Operations University Press, August).

Greengard, S. 2015. *The Internet of Things* (Cambridge, MA: MIT Press).

Groll, E. 2016. 'U.S. spy chiefs think the world is pretty much going to hell', *Foreign Policy* (9 February).

Gruszczak, A. 2016. *Intelligence Security in the European Union: Building a Strategic Intelligence Community* (London: Springer).

Guldi, J., and D. Armitage (2014 [rev. 2015]). *The History Manifesto* (Cambridge: Cambridge University Press).

Hall, W.M., and G. Citrenbaum. 2010. *Intelligence Analysis* (Santa Barbara, CA: Praeger Security International).

———. 2012. *Intelligence Collection* (Santa Barbara, CA: Praeger Security International).

Hamaid, M. 2015. 'Social media intelligence: Successes, challenges, and future prospects', *Journal of the Australian Institute of Professional Intelligence Officers*, 23, 3, pp. 3–21.

Hamid, S. 2016. 'Donald Trump and the authoritarian temptation', Brookings Institution (9 May).

Hammes, T.X. 2016. 'Will technological convergence reverse globalization?', *US National Defense University Strategic Forum* (July).

Handel, M.I. 2001. 'Deception, surprise, and intelligence', ch. 15 in M.I. Handel, *Masters of War*, 3rd ed. (London: Routledge).

Harding, L. 2014. *The Snowden Files* (London: Guardian Faber).

Hare, N., and P. Coghill. 2016. 'The future of the intelligence analysis task', *Intelligence and National Security* (January).

Hargreaves, J. 2016. 'Why both sides are wrong in the counter-extremism debate', *The Conversation* (3 March).

Hastedt, G. 2013. 'Book review: "Understanding the globalization of intelligence", Adam N. [*sic*] M. Svendsen', *Journal of Contingencies and Crisis Management*, 21, 2 (June), pp. 125–6.

Hayden, M.V. 2016. *Playing to the Edge: American Intelligence in the Age of Terror* (New York: Penguin).

Hayes, W. 2015. 'The dark side of big data', *Forbes* (14 September).

Heuer, R. 1999. *Psychology of Intelligence Analysis* (Washington, DC: CIA Center for the Study of Intelligence).

Heuer, R.J. Jr., and R.H. Pherson. 2014. *Structured Analytic Techniques for Intelligence Analysis*, 2nd ed. (Washington, DC: CQ Press).

Hill, F. 2016. 'Putin: The one-man show the West doesn't understand', *Bulletin of the Atomic Scientists*, 72, 3.

Hobbs, C., M. Moran, and D. Salisbury, eds. 2014. *Open Source Intelligence in the Twenty-First Century: New Approaches and Opportunities* (Basingstoke, UK: Palgrave Macmillan).

Howarth, D. 2013. *Law as Engineering : Thinking About What Lawyers Do* (Cheltenham, UK: Edward Elgar).

Ingram, H.J. 2016. 'An analysis of *Inspire* and *Dabiq*: Lessons from AQAP and Islamic State's propaganda war', *Studies in Conflict & Terrorism* (13 July).

Jackson, C.F. 2016. 'Information is not a weapons system', *Journal of Strategic Studies* (7 March).

James, A. 2013. *Examining Intelligence-Led Policing: Developments in Research, Policy and Practice* (Basingstoke, UK: Palgrave Macmillan).

———. 2016. *Understanding Police Intelligence Work* (Bristol, UK: Policy Press).

Jang, J., J. McSparren, and Y. Rashchupkina. 2016. 'Global governance: Present and future', *Palgrave Communications*, 2, 15045.

Jeffrey Smith, R. 2016. 'Nuclear security: A vital goal but a distant prospect', *Center for Public Integrity* (28 March).

Jeffreys-Jones, R. 2013. *In Spies We Trust: The Story of Western Intelligence* (Oxford: Oxford University Press).

Jervis, R. 2010. *Why Intelligence Fails* (Ithaca, NY: Cornell University Press).

Johnson, L.K., and M. Phythian. 2016. 'Intelligence and national security at thirty', *Intelligence and National Security*, 31, 1, pp. 1–7.

Johnson, L.K., and J.J. Wirtz, eds. 2014. *Intelligence: The Secret World of Spies—An Anthology*, 4th ed. (Oxford: Oxford University Press).

Jones, R.V. 1978. *Most Secret War: British Scientific Intelligence 1939–45* (London: Hamish Hamilton).

Jordan, D., J.D. Kiras, D.J. Lonsdale, I. Speller, C. Tuck, and C.D. Walton. 2016. *Understanding Modern Warfare*, 2nd ed. (Cambridge: Cambridge University Press).

Kasriel, T. 2012. *Futurescaping: Business Insight to Plan Your Life* (London: Bloomsbury).

Kaunert, C., and S. Leonard, eds. 2013. *European Security, Terrorism, and Intelligence: Tackling New Security Challenges in Europe* (Basingstoke, UK: Palgrave Macmillan).

Kahneman, D. 2011. *Thinking, Fast and Slow* (London: Allen Lane).

Kilcullen, D. 2013. *Out of the Mountains: The Coming Age of the Urban Guerrilla* (London: Hurst).

Kirkpatrick, J. 2016. 'Interview—Amitav Acharya', ISN/ETHZ/e-IR.info (April).

Klausen, J., T. Morrill, and R. Libretti. 2016. 'The terrorist age-crime curve: An analysis of American Islamist terrorist offenders and age-specific propensity for participation in violent and nonviolent incidents', *Social Science Quarterly*, 97, pp. 19–32.

Kringen, J.A. 2015. 'Keeping watch on the world: Rethinking the concept of global coverage in the US intelligence community', *CIA Studies in Intelligence*, 59, 3 (September), pp. 1–10.

Kruithof, K., J. Aldridge, D. Décary Hétu, M. Sim, E. Dujso, and S. Hoorens. 2016. 'The role of the "dark web" in the trade of illicit drugs', *Rand Europe Brief*.

Lahneman, W.J., and R. Arcos, eds. 2014. *The Art of Intelligence: Simulations, Exercises, and Games* (Lanham, MD: Rowman & Littlefield).

Landau, S. 2011. *Surveillance or Security?* (Cambridge, MA: MIT Press).

Larson, E.V. et al. 2008. *Assessing Irregular Warfare: A Framework for Intelligence Analysis* (Rand Corporation).

Laverick, W. 2016. *Global Injustice and Crime Control* (London: Routledge).

Lewis, B.A. 2016. 'The death of human intelligence: How human intelligence has been minimized since the 1960s', *Military & Strategic Affairs*, 8, 1 (July).

Lichacz, F.M.J., and R. Jassemi-Zargani. 2016. *Human Factors and Intelligence, Surveillance, and Reconnaissance (ISR): Making the case for a Human Factors Capability in the ISR Concept Development & Evaluation (CD&E) Process* (Ottawa, Canada: Defence Research and Development Canada—Ottawa Research Centre).

Lim, K. 2015. 'Big data and strategic intelligence', *Intelligence and National Security*.

Lockwood, J.S. 2013. *The Lockwood Analytical Method for Prediction (LAMP): A Method for Predictive Intelligence Analysis* (London: Bloomsbury Intelligence Studies).

Lowe, D. 2014. 'Surveillance and international terrorism intelligence exchange: Balancing the interests of national security and individual liberty', *Terrorism and Political Violence* (August).

Lowenthal, M.M. 2015. *Intelligence: From Secrets to Policy*, 6th ed. (Washington, DC: CQ Press).

Lowenthal, M.M., and R.M. Clark. 2015. *The Five Disciplines of Intelligence Collection* (Washington, DC: CQ Press).

Lynch, C. 2016. 'Fearing Trump, U.N. embraces the art of the deal', *Foreign Policy* (28 March).

Lyon, D. 2007. *Surveillance Studies* (Cambridge: Polity).

Lysgård, A., 2016. 'The evolution of the global SOF enterprise from a partner perspective', *Joint Special Operations University Occasional Paper* (MacDill AFB, FL: Joint Special Operations University, October).

MacCalman, M. 2016. 'A.Q. Khan nuclear smuggling network', *Journal of Strategic Security*, 9, 1, pp. 104–18.

Madden, D. et al. 2016. *Toward Operational Art in Special Warfare* (Santa Monica, CA: Rand Corporation).

Magney, N. 2016. 'CONTEST, prevent, and the lessons of UK counterterrorism policy', *Georgetown Security Studies Review* (16 May).

Malone, T.W., and M.S. Bernstein, eds. 2015. *Handbook of Collective Intelligence* (Cambridge, MA: MIT Press).

Marrin, S. 2012. 'Is intelligence analysis an art or a science?', *International Journal of Intelligence and CounterIntelligence*, 25, 3.

——. 2013. 'Revisiting intelligence and policy: Problems with politicization and receptivity', *Intelligence and National Security*, 28, 1.

May, C. 2015. 'Who's in charge? Corporations as institutions of global governance', *Palgrave Communications*, 1, 15042.

Mayer-Schönberger, V., and K. Cukier. 2013. *Big Data: A Revolution That Will Transform How We Live, Work and Think* (London: John Murray).

——. 2013. 'The rise of big data: How it's changing the way we think about the world', *Foreign Affairs* (May/June).

Mazarr, M.J. 2016. *Rethinking Risk in National Security: Lessons of the Financial Crisis for Risk Management* (Basingstoke, UK: Palgrave Macmillan).

McCarthy, N. 2009. *Engineering* (London: Oneworld).

McLery, P., and D. De Luce. 2016. 'Exclusive: Top House lawmaker accuses Pentagon of obstructing intel probe', *Foreign Policy* (26 February).

Mendosa, J.A. 2016. 'Operations-driven intelligence: Is the shirt on backwards?' *International Journal of Intelligence and CounterIntelligence*, 29, 4, pp. 677–99.

Mintz, A., and C. Wayne. 2016. 'The polythink syndrome and elite group decision-making', *Political Psychology*, 37.

Mitchell, W.L. 2014. 'Building a componential Danish SOF for a global SOF network', *FAK Brief* (Copenhagen: Royal Danish Defence College).

Monaghan, A. 2016. 'No going back to business as usual for NATO and Russia', *Chatham House Commentary* (25 April).

Moran, C. 2015. *Company Confessions: Revealing CIA Secrets* (London: Biteback).

Moran, J. 2016. 'Assessing SOF transparency and accountability', *Remote Control Report—Oxford Research Group* (4 July).

Nissen, T.E. 2015. *#TheWeaponizationOfSocialMedia* (Copenhagen: Royal Danish Defence College).

Normandin, J-M., and M-C. Therrien. 2016. 'Resilience factors reconciled with complexity: The dynamics of order and Disorder', *Journal of Contingencies and Crisis Management*.

O'Malley, P. 2015. 'Revisiting the classics: "Policing the risk society" in the twenty-first century', *Policing and Society*, 25, 4, pp. 426–31.

ODNI. 2014. *National Intelligence Strategy (NIS) of the United States of America 2014* (Washington, DC).

Olsen, J.A., ed. 2015. *Airpower Reborn: The Strategic Concepts of John Warden and John Boyd* (Annapolis, MD: Naval Institute Press).

Omand, D., J. Bartlett, and C. Miller. 2012. 'Introducing social media intelligence (SOCMINT)', *Intelligence and National Security*, 27, 6 (September), pp. 801–823.

Omand, D. 2014. 'Understanding Bayesian thinking: Prior and posterior probabilities and analysis of competing hypotheses in intelligence analysis', ch. 12 in Lahneman and Arcos, eds. *The Art of Intelligence*.

Osinga, F.P.B. 2007. *Science, Strategy and War: The Strategic Theory of John Boyd* (London: Routledge).

Osinga, F. 2016. 'Organizing for insecurity and chaos: Resilience and modern military theory', chapter 3 in R. Beeres, G. Bak, E. de Waard, and S. Rietjens, eds., *NL ARMS Netherlands Annual Review of Military Studies 2016: Organizing for Safety and Security in Military Organizations* (The Hague: Asser Press/Springer).

Palacios, J-M. 2016. 'Intelligence analysis training: A European perspective', *International Journal of Intelligence, Security, and Public Affairs*, 18, 1, pp. 34–56.

Patman, R.G., and L. Southgate. 2015. 'National security and surveillance: The public impact of the GCSB Amendment Bill and the Snowden revelations in New Zealand', *Intelligence and National Security*.

Paul, C., and M. Matthews. 2016. 'The Russian "firehose of falsehood" propaganda model: Why it might work and options to counter it', *Rand Perspective*.

Peake, H. 2015. 'Intelligence officer's bookshelf —Special: A spectrum of views on the use of drones', *CIA Studies in Intelligence*, 59, 4 (December).

Pecht, E., and A. Tishler. 2015. 'Budget allocation, national security, military intelligence, and human capital: A dynamic model', *Defence and Peace Economics* (November).

Perkins, D.G. 2016. 'Big picture, not details, key when eyeing future', *Army Magazine* (12 April).

Perry, D.L. 2016. *Ethics in War, Espionage, Covert Action, and Interrogation*, 2nd ed. (Lanham, MD: Rowman & Littlefield).

Perry, W.L., B. McInnis, C.C. Price, S. Smith, and J.S. Hollywood. 2013. *Predictive Policing: The Role of Crime Forecasting in Law Enforcement Operations* (Santa Monica, CA: Rand Corporation).

Pham, C. 2014. 'Effectiveness of metadata information and tools applied to national security', *Library Philosophy and Practice*, 1077.

Phillips, M.D. 2016. 'Time series applications to intelligence analysis: A case study of homicides in Mexico', *Intelligence and National Security*, 31, 5, pp. 729–45.

Pincus, W. 2016. 'Reflections on secrecy and the press from a life in journalism', *National Security, Technology, and Law—Hoover Institution Essay, Series Paper no. 1602.*

Pollack, K.M. 2016. 'Security and public order', *Brookings Report* (February).

Pomerantz, J. 2015. *Metadata* (Cambridge, MA: MIT Press).

Porche, I.R. III, 2016. 'Emerging cyber threats and Implications', *Testimony presented before the House Homeland Security Committee, Subcommittee on Cybersecurity, Infrastructure Protection, and Security Technologies* (Washington, DC: Rand Corporation).

Posner, E.A. 2009. *The Perils of Global Legalism* (Chicago: University of Chicago Press).

Post, R., and J.D. Peterson. 2016. *Unconventional Economics: Operational Economics in Unconventional Warfare* (MacDill, FL: Joint Special Operations University Press).

Powell, A. 2016. 'Advice from SOF on the use of SOF for the next Administration', *CNA Report* (Washington, DC).

Pressman, D.E. 2009. 'Risk assessment decisions for violent political extremism 2009–02' (Ottawa: Public Safety Canada), www.publicsafety.gc.ca/cnt/rsrcs/pblctns/2009-02-rdv/index-en.aspx.

Priest, G. 2000. *Logic: A Very Short Introduction* (Oxford: Oxford University Press).

Public Safety Canada. 2009. 'Assessing the risk of violent extremists', *Research Summary*, 14, 5 (September).

Pynnöniemi, K., and A. Rácz. eds. 2016. *Fog of Falsehood: Russian Strategy of Deception and the Conflict in Ukraine* (Helsinki: Finnish Institute of International Affairs).

Quarmby, N. 2003. 'Futures work in strategic criminal intelligence', conference paper (Canberra, Australia).

Ratcliffe, J.H. 2016. *Intelligence-Led Policing*, 2nd ed. (London: Routledge).

Ravndal, J.A. 2009. 'Developing intelligence capabilities in support of UN peace operations', *NUPI Report* (December).

Reeve, R., and T. Street. 2016. 'Brexit: Whither UK defence and foreign policy?', *Oxford Research Group Briefing* (July).

Renz, B. 2016. 'Why Russia is reviving its conventional military power', *Parameters*, 46, 2, pp. 23–36.

Reveron, D.S., and J.L. Cook. 2013. 'From national to theater: Developing strategy', *Joint Forces Quarterly*, 70, pp. 113–20.

Richards, J. 2010. *The Art and Science of Intelligence Analysis* (Oxford: Oxford University Press).

———. 2014. 'Competing hypotheses in contemporary intelligence Analysis', ch. 2 in Lahneman and Arcos, eds., *The Art of Intelligence.*

———. 2016. 'Intelligence studies, academia and professionalization', *International Journal of Intelligence, Security, and Public Affairs*, 18, 1, pp. 20–33.

Richardson, S., and N. Gilmour. 2016. *Intelligence and Security Oversight: An Annotated Bibliography and Comparative Analysis* (Basingstoke, UK: Palgrave Pivot).

Robinson, L. 2013. *One Hundred Victories: Special Ops and the Future of American Warfare* (New York: Public Affairs).

————. 2015. 'ISIS vs special ops: One half of a good strategy', *Foreign Affairs* (7 December).

Rodin, J. 2015. *The Resilience Dividend* (London: Profile).

Rovner, J. 2011. 'Faulty intelligence', *Foreign Policy* (22 June).

————. 2011. *Fixing the Facts: National Security and the Politics of Intelligence* (Ithaka, NY: Cornell University Press).

Russell, S., and P. Norvig. 2016. *Artificial Intelligence: A Modern Approach*, 3rd ed. (Harlow, UK: Pearson).

Rutkowski, A.M. 2016. 'International signals intelligence law: Provisions and history', *Lawfare Research Papers Series*, 4, 1 (March).

Sambei, A. 2013. 'Intelligence cooperation versus evidence collection and dissemination', ch. 7 in L. van den Herik and N. Schrijver, eds., *Counter-terrorism Strategies in a Fragmented International Legal Order: Meeting the Challenges* (Cambridge: Cambridge University Press), pp. 212–39.

Schroefl, J., B.M. Rajaee, and D. Muhr, eds. 2011. *Hybrid and Cyber War as Consequences of the Asymmetry* (Frankfurt: Peter Lang International).

Segell, G. 2012. 'Book review: International intelligence cooperation and accountability', *Political Studies Review*, 10, 3, pp. 410–11.

Shea, J. 2016. 'Resilience: A core element of collective defence', *NATO Review* (April).

Sheffi, Y. 2015. *The Power of Resilience* (Cambridge, MA: MIT Press).

Shiraz, Z. 2013. 'Drugs and dirty wars: Intelligence cooperation in the global South', *Third World Quarterly*, 34, 10.

Silver, N. 2012. *The Signal and the Noise* (London: Allen Lane).

Simpson, E. 2012. *War From the Ground Up: Twenty-First Century Combat as Politics* (London: Hurst).

Sinclair Cotter, R. 2015. 'Police intelligence: Connecting-the-dots in a network society', *Policing and Society* (June).

Smith, R. 2006. *The Utility of Force: The Art of War in the Modern World* (London: Penguin).

Snyder, T. 2016. 'The wars of Vladimir Putin', *New York Review of Books* (9 June).

Soufan, A. 2015. 'Did Iran give up the Khobar Towers terrorist?' *Foreign Policy* (8 September).

Stern, J., and J.M. Berger. 2016. *ISIS: The State of Terror* (London: Collins).

Stewart, B., and S. Newbery. 2015. *Why Spy? The Art of Intelligence* (London: Hurst).

Stoddart, K. 2016. 'UK cyber security and critical national infrastructure protection', *International Affairs*, 92, 5, pp. 1079–1105.

Strachan, H. 2013. *The Direction of War: Contemporary Strategy In Historical Perspective* (Cambridge: Cambridge University Press).

Sutherland B.J., ed. 2011. *Modern Warfare, Intelligence and Deterrence* (London: John Wiley).

Svendsen, A.D.M. 2008. 'The globalization of intelligence since 9/11: Frameworks and operational parameters', *Cambridge Review of International Affairs*, 21, 1.

————. 2008. 'The globalization of intelligence since 9/11: The optimization of intelligence liaison arrangements', *International Journal of Intelligence and Counter-Intelligence*, 21, 4 (December), pp. 661–78.

———. 2009. 'Painting rather than photography: Exploring spy fiction as a legitimate source concerning UK–US intelligence co-operation', *Journal of Transatlantic Studies*, 7, 1.

———. 2009. 'Connecting intelligence and theory: Intelligence liaison and international relations', *Intelligence and National Security*, 24, 5 (October).

———. 2010. 'Strategy and disproportionality in contemporary conflicts', *Journal of Strategic Studies*, 33, 3 (June).

———. 2010. 'Re-fashioning risk: Comparing UK, US and Canadian security and intelligence efforts against terrorism', *Defence Studies*, 10, 3 (September), pp. 307–35.

———. 2010. *Intelligence Cooperation and the War on Terror: Anglo-American Security Relations after 9/11* (London: Routledge).

———. 2011. 'On "a continuum with expansion"? Intelligence co-operation in Europe in the early twenty-first century', *Journal of Contemporary European Research*, 7, 4, pp. 520–38.

———. 2011. 'NATO, Libya operations and intelligence co-operation—A step forward?' *Baltic Security & Defence Review*, 13, 2 (December).

———. 2012. 'The Federal Bureau of Investigation and change: Addressing US domestic counter-terrorism intelligence', *Intelligence and National Security*, 27, 3 (June).

———. 2012. '"Strained" relations? Evaluating contemporary Anglo-American intelligence and security co-operation', ch. 8 in S. Marsh and A. Dobson, eds., *Anglo-American Relations: Contemporary Perspectives* (London: Routledge).

———. 2012. *Understanding the Globalization of Intelligence* (Basingstoke, UK: Palgrave Macmillan).

———. 2012. *The Professionalization of Intelligence Cooperation: Fashioning Method Out of Mayhem* (Basingstoke, UK: Palgrave Macmillan).

———. 2013. 'Introducing RESINT: A "missing" and "undervalued" INT in all-source intelligence efforts', *International Journal of Intelligence and Counterintelligence*, 26, 4, pp. 777–94.

———. 2013. 'On "a continuum with expansion"? Intelligence co-operation in Europe in the early Twenty-first Century', in Kaunert and Leonard, eds., *European Security, Terrorism, and Intelligence*.

———. 2013. '1968—"A year to remember" for the study of British Intelligence?' chapter in C.R. Moran and C.J. Murphy, eds., *Intelligence Studies in Britain and the US: Historiography since 1945* (Edinburgh: Edinburgh University Press).

———. 2014. 'Buffeted not busted: The UKUSA "five eyes" after Snowden', e-ir. info, www.e-ir.info/2014/01/08/buffeted-not-busted-the-ukusa-five-eyes-after-snowden/ (July 2016).

———. 2014. 'Sharpening SOF tools, their strategic use and direction: Optimising the command of special operations amid wider contemporary defence transformation and military cuts', *Defence Studies*, 14, 3, pp. 284–309.

———. 2014. 'Collective intelligence (COLINT)', in G. Moore, ed., *Encyclopedia of U.S. Intelligence* (New York: CRC Press).

———. 2015. 'Advancing "defence-in-depth": Intelligence and systems dynamics', *Defense & Security Analysis*, 31, 1, pp. 58–73.

———. 2015. 'Contemporary intelligence innovation in practice: Enhancing "macro" to "micro" systems thinking via "System of Systems" dynamics', *Defence Studies*, 15, 2, pp. 105–23.

———. 2015. 'Intelligence liaison', *Intelligencer—US Association of Former Intelligence Officers* (May).

———. 2015. '"Smart law" for intelligence!' *Tech & Law Center* (June).

———. 2015. '"Making it STARC"! Proposed future ways forward for contemporary military & special operations intelligence & knowledge work'. Conference paper. *International Symposium on Military Operational Research (ISMOR) 2015*. Royal Holloway, University of London.

———. 2015. 'Advancing system of systems dynamics (SoSD) in the cyber intelligence (CYBINT) domain'. Conference paper. *International Society of Military Sciences 2015*. Finnish Defence University, Helsinki.

———. 2015. 'Making arms control "smarter"? The importance of intelligence', *Utrikes Perspektiv* (October).

———. 2016. 'Developing international intelligence liaison against Islamic State: Approaching "one for all and all for one"?' *International Journal of Intelligence and CounterIntelligence*, 29, 2.

———. 2016. 'An intelligence-engineering framework for defence engagement considerations'. Conference paper. *Human Geography in Defence Engagement: 9th Annual International Spatial Socio-Cultural Knowledge Workshop*. UK Defence Academy, Shrivenham, UK.

———. 2016. 'Extending the academy: Advancing functional intelligence studies (FIS)'. Conference paper. *International Association for Intelligence Education (IAFIE). 12th Annual* Conference. Breda, NL.

———. 2016. 'Teaching an intelligence-based framework for risk'. Conference paper. *International Association for Intelligence Education (IAFIE), 12th Annual Conference*. Breda, NL.

———. 2016. 'Discovering "unknown-unknowns" & beyond'. Conference paper. *33rd International Symposium on Military Operational Research*. Royal Holloway, University of London.

———. 2016. 'International intelligence liaison: A primer', *Romanian Journal of Intelligence Studies*.

———. Forthcoming. 'Strategic futures and intelligence: The head and heart of "hybrid defence" providing tangible meaning and ways forward'.

———. Forthcoming. 'Intelligence, surveillance and reconnaissance (ISR)', in J. Deni and D. Galbreath, eds., *The Routledge Handbook of Defence Studies* (London: Routledge).

Symon, P.B., and A. Tarapore. 2015. 'Defense intelligence analysis in the age of big data', *Joint Forces Quarterly*, 79, pp. 4–11.

Takeyh, R. 2016. 'America will regret abandoning the Middle East', *Foreign Policy* (3 May).

Tecuci, G., D.A. Schum, D. Marcu, and M. Boicu. 2016. *Intelligence Analysis as Discovery of Evidence, Hypotheses, and Arguments: Connecting the Dots* (Cambridge: Cambridge University Press).

Thakur, R. 2016. 'The responsibility to protect at 15', *International Affairs*, 92, pp. 415–34.

Thomson, J. 2015. 'Governance costs and defence intelligence provision in the UK: A case-study in microeconomic theory', *Intelligence and National Security*.

Tikk-Ringas, E. ed. 2015. *Evolution of the Cyber Domain: The Implications for National and Global Security* (London: IISS Strategic Dossier).

Treverton, G.F., and T.M. Sanderson. 2016. 'Strategic intelligence: A view from the National Intelligence Council (NIC)'. Center for Strategic and International Studies (Washington, DC: 4 March).

Tromblay, D.E. 2015. 'The threat review and prioritization trap: How the FBI's new threat review and prioritization process compounds the Bureau's oldest problems', *Intelligence and National Security*.

Osborne, P. 2016. 'Defence intelligence: Increasingly different today and tomorrow'. Video. Royal United Services Institute for Defence and Security Studies (1 March).

UK HM Government. 2016. 'Data science ethical framework', *Cabinet Office Publication* (19 May).

UK Ministry of Defence. 2013. *Red Teaming Guide*, 2nd ed. (Shrivenham, UK: Development, Concepts and Doctrine Centre, UK Defence Academy, March).

UK Ministry of Defence. 2014. *Global Strategic Trends out to 2045*, 5th ed. (Shrivenham, UK: Development, Concepts and Doctrine Centre).

U.S. Information Sharing Environment. 2016. 'JCAT releases 2016 intelligence guide for first responders', *ISE Bulletin* (14 March).

———. 2016. 'Criminal Intelligence Coordinating Council (CICC) helps law enforcement share information and intelligence to prevent crime and terrorism', *Information Sharing Environment Office Weekly Digest Bulletin* (3 April).

U.S. Joint Chiefs of Staff. 2011. *Joint Publication J-P 3.0* (August).

U.S. Office of the Director of National Intelligence. 2013. *U.S. National Intelligence: An Overview 2013* (Washington, DC: April).

Van Buuren, J. 2014. 'From oversight to undersight: The internationalization of intelligence', *Security & Human Rights*.

Velasco, F. 2016. 'Editorial', *International Journal of Intelligence, Security, and Public Affairs*, 18, 1, pp. 1–4.

Ven Bruusgaard, K. 2016. 'Russian strategic deterrence', *Survival*, 58, 4, pp. 7–26.

Von Rosing, M., H. von Scheel, A-W. Scheer, and A.D.M. Svendsen et al. 2014. 'Business process trends', chapter in M. von Rosing, H. von Scheel, and A-W. Scheer, eds., *The Complete Business Process Handbook—Volume 1* (Burlington, MA: Morgan Kaufmann/Elsevier).

Vrist Rønn, K. 2016. 'Intelligence ethics: A critical review and future perspectives', *International Journal of Intelligence and CounterIntelligence*, 29, 4, pp. 760–84.

Waddell, A.P. 2015. 'Cooperation and integration among Australia's national security community', *CIA Studies in Intelligence*, 59, 3 (September). pp. 25–34.

Wagner, D., and D. Disparte. 2016. *Global Risk Agility and Decision Making: Organizational Resilience in the Era of Man-Made Risk* (London: Springer).

Walsh, P.F. 2011. *Intelligence and Intelligence Analysis* (London: Routledge).

Walsh, P.F., and S. Miller. 2015. 'Rethinking "five eyes" security intelligence collection policies and practice post-Snowden', *Intelligence and National Security*.

Warner, M. 2012. 'Cybersecurity: A pre-history', *Intelligence and National Security*, 27, 5, pp. 781–99.

Warrick, J. 2015. *Black Flags: The Rise of ISIS* (London: Bantam).

Weatherall, J.O. 2014. *The Physics of Finance—Predicting the Unpredictable: How Science Has Taken Over Wall Street* (London: Short Books).

Wirtz, J.J. 2016. *Understanding Intelligence Failure: Warning, Response and Deterrence* (London: Routledge).

Young, W., and D. Stebbins. 2016. 'A rapidly changing urban environment: How commercial technologies can affect military intelligence operations', *Rand Perspective* (Santa Monica, CA: Rand Corporation).

Zegart, A., and S.D. Krasner, eds. 2015. *Pragmatic Engagement Amidst Global Uncertainty: Three Major Challenges* (Washington, DC: Hoover Institution).

Zwitter, A. 2016. *Humanitarian Intelligence: A Practitioner's Guide to Crisis Analysis and Project Design* (Lanham, MD: Rowman & Littlefield).

Ångström, J., and J.J. Widén. 2015. *Contemporary Military Theory: The Dynamics of War* (London: Routledge).

Index

#2 Intelligence (e.g., G/J2), 5, 21, 25, 60–63, 66–67, 72. *See also* intelligence
#3 Operations (e.g., G/J3), 5, 21, 25, 60, 62, 63, 67, 72. *See also* operations
'3Rs', 62, 74. *See also* STARC criteria
'4Vs', 22, 82n43

a priori, 25, 74, 87. *See also* post facto
A + B + C factors, 89, 91. *See also* key actors, forces/factors of change, possible change over time
academic, 3, 39, 66, 111n24, 113n30, 128
accountability, 11n10, 22, 78n15, 89, 126
adaption, 86, 92, 93, 104, 106
agility, 86, 105, 109n18, 132
air (domain), 18, 21, 28n13, 44, 62. *See also* M4IS2
all-source, 5, 18, 67. *See also* multiple intelligence disciplines (multi-INTs)
analyses, 23, 102
analysts, 3, 5, 7, 11n11, 38, 39, 40, 50n36, 59, 66, 95n9, 100, 102, 121
analytic continuity, 86

Anglo-American intelligence and security interactions, 3, 4, 8n3, 123, 130. *See also* UKUSA relations
art, vii, 14n16, 24, 27n10, 37–39, 42, 43, 47n1–9, 47n11–12, 47n14, 48n17, 77n15, 80n33, 101, 110n20, 125, 126, 127, 128, 129
artificial intelligence (AI), 20, 27n10, 50n39, 54n51, 119, 129
artistic, 19, 37, 38, 41, 46, 100. *See also* creativity

backdoor access, 22, 31n20
balancing, 4, 22, 23, 24, 37, 41, 42, 48n24, 82n46, 89, 106, 112n26, 113n30, 125
battlespaces, 21, 60, 65, 70, 87
behaviour, 37, 38, 39, 42, 87
'best practices', 45, 54n52, 73
'big data', 22, 30n18, 31n19, 32n22, 49n24, 55n56, 74, 76n8, 82n43, 120, 124, 125, 126, 131
'big picture', 18, 23, 42, 60, 81n35, 127
Blockley, David, 19, 26n8, 42, 49n28, 120
blowback, 25, 35n32, 106

About the Author

Adam D.M. Svendsen (PhD, University of Warwick, UK) is an international intelligence and defence strategist, educator, researcher, analyst and consultant—twitter: @intstrategist

Among many roles, he is a co-founder and co-director of the Bridgehead Institute (research & consulting) and an associate consultant at the Copenhagen Institute for Futures Studies (CIFS), Denmark. He works as a strategic intelligence and risk consultant, having trained at European defence and emergency planning colleges, lectured at the senior and advanced levels at the Royal Danish Defence College (FAK), given guest lectures at the Royal Netherlands Defence Academy, and taught at the University of Nottingham.

He divides his time between the UK and Scandinavia, helping to advise on both national and regional (European) projects, while contributing to the research work of various countries' defence research agencies and intelligence academies as well as towards the efforts of international organisations such as the United Nations.

He has been a visiting scholar at the Center for Peace and Security Studies, Georgetown University; has held a post-doctoral fellowship with the Centre for Military Studies (CMS), Department of Political Science, University of Copenhagen, Denmark; has worked at Chatham House on the International Security Programme; and has also worked at the International Institute for Strategic Studies in London.

Together with work cited in testimony to the Foreign Affairs Committee of the British Parliament and participating in the RUSI Strategic Hub on Organised Crime Research, he has multi-sector, award-winning, international media and communication experience, and he is the author of numerous articles and chapters as well as three other books: *Intelligence Cooperation and the War on Terror: Anglo-American Security Relations after 9/11* (2010); *Understanding the Globalization of Intelligence* (2012); and *The Professionalization of Intelligence Cooperation: Fashioning Method Out of Mayhem* (2012).